TEACHERS
of COLOR

TEACHERS
of COLOR
RESISTING RACISM
AND RECLAIMING
EDUCATION

RITA KOHLI

Harvard Education Press
Cambridge, Massachusetts

Second Printing, 2021

Paperback ISBN 978-1-68253-637-7

Library Edition ISBN 978-1-68253-638-4

Library of Congress Cataloging-in-Publication data is on file.

Published by Harvard Education Press,
an imprint of the Harvard Education Publishing Group

Harvard Education Press
8 Story Street
Cambridge, MA 02138

Cover Design: Endpaper Studio
Cover Image: iStock.com/Lyubov Ivanova

The typefaces used in this book are Adobe Garamond Pro, Gotham, and Surveyor Fine

This book is dedicated in loving memory to my grandmothers and ancestors: Prem Lata Mehta, who committed her life to creating a better and more just education for her community and whose legacy continues to impact so many; and Kamla Devi Kohli, who had little access to formal education and embodied so much intelligence and power through her wit, wisdom, and love.

CONTENTS

Series Foreword

by H. Richard Milner IV
Race and Education Series Editor

Teachers of Color: Resisting Racism and Reclaiming Education is just the book we need at a time in the United States when our teaching force has far too few teachers of Color. Following the *Brown v. Board of Education* decision in 1954, the US lost an enormous number of teachers of Color to the detriment of the social, affective, behavioral, and academic success of students, particularly students of Color.[1] Rita Kohli places front and center the ways in which hostile, racist school climates push teachers out of the teaching pipeline and profession. Importantly, Kohli documents powerful racialized intersections of schooling experiences among people of Color with the working conditions of educators of Color. In short, our educational system, institutions, and structures play a significant role in attrition among teachers of Color. Drawing from her rich and robust research, Kohli documents complex dynamics of educational and institutional racism and their effects on teachers of Color.

Kohli not only exceptionally advances the real issues underlying why racism is still so prevalent in schools and educational systems, and the profound influences of racism, prejudice, and other forms of discrimination on the decisions of teachers of Color to enter or remain in the profession, but also provides insights into the structures, systems, and experiences that propel these teachers' perseverance. What does it take to support teachers of Color to succeed and build equitable, necessary educational ecologies? How might professional learning opportunities support teachers of Color and other educators in recognizing the ways in which systemic racism perpetuates and maintains the status quo, whiteness, and white supremacy? What can teacher education programs do to better support the learning and developmental needs of teachers to recognize and reimagine educational environments of justice?

Too often, school districts cite the teacher of Color pipeline (the low numbers of teachers of Color) for their inability to diversify their teaching faculty. This book provides compelling arguments to more deeply interrogate trends in teacher demographics to understand how teachers of Color are opting out or pushed out due to ingrained sources of racism and discrimination. To be sure, school districts (teachers, counselors, leaders, boards, and coaches alike) can learn from this book and radically reimagine and transform their policies and practices to build a teaching force for equity and justice. Perhaps most importantly, this book provides groundbreaking recommendations and implications for building a teacher of Color pipeline representative of the racially and ethnically diverse students in US schools.

Teachers of Color poignantly identifies the relevance of race and details recommendations for increasing, retaining, and honoring teachers of Color as we work to build anti-racist policy, practices, and innovation. A welcome addition to the Race and Education Series, this book is needed in our field!

FOREWORD

I FIRST MET RITA KOHLI at the annual meeting of the American Educational Research Association (AERA) in San Diego, California, where we had a conversation about the state of urban schools and the everyday experiences of students and teachers of Color. We talked about various theoretical and methodological frameworks she and I had been using to wrestle with and advance racial justice. Rita explained that she had been a resource teacher in the Oakland Unified School District and had also served students from New York City Public Schools to San Diego City Schools, both in the classroom and with their college and career goals. At some point in the conversation, she told me she wanted to pursue her PhD working with me at UCLA, and in the fall of 2004, she began the doctoral program in the Graduate School of Education and Information Studies in social science and comparative education with a specialization in race and ethnic studies. I was Rita's adviser and soon her dissertation chair, and four years later, she completed her dissertation, "Breaking the Cycle of Racism in the Classroom: Critical Race Reflections of Women of Color Educators."[1]

I share this story because it shows Rita's long commitment to racial justice and educational equity. Her experiences in teaching and working with K–12 students, in the doctoral program at UCLA, and as a professor of education both at San José State University and now at the University of California, Riverside, have all contributed to this book, *Teachers of Color: Resisting Racism and Reclaiming Education.*

In the sixteen years Rita and I have worked together, we have traded many stories about our lives as teachers, researchers, and activists. She recently reminded me of my own teaching origin story—especially as it relates to this book. I was born, raised, and went to Catholic schools in a Mexican and Italian working-class community called Lincoln Heights, just east of downtown Los Angeles. I continued on to get my undergraduate degree in sociology and Mexican American studies at Loyola University in 1972. The summer after graduation, I became a high school social studies teacher at the Los Angeles County Central Juvenile Hall School—a youth correctional facility. I was part of a program called the National Teacher Corps, one of the first federally funded teacher training programs to prepare educators to work in urban and rural underserved communities of Color, and the year I participated the program's focus was on urban corrections. As a first-year novice teacher, this is where I found the work of Brazilian educator and critical social theorist Paulo Freire. In our classrooms, with an amazing group of other Teacher Corps interns, we worked together to engage the students in what Freire refers to as "reading the word" and "reading the world." Freire's three general phases of problem-posing pedagogy include identifying and naming the problem, analyzing the causes of the problem, and finding solutions to the problem.[2] To create a liberating education for my students, I used a variation of this method, in which two-way dialogues of cooperation, respect, and action between the student and teacher became the focus, content, and pedagogy of the classroom.

We began "naming the problem" by engaging in dialogue about injustice in the worlds students came from—mostly South Central and East Los Angeles. In those discussions, I asked students to tell me about their communities and the people, places, and things that were important to them. Their communities were the ones I grew up in, journeyed through, and worked in during my adolescent and adult life. After school and on weekends, I traveled and took photographs of people, places, and things they mentioned. These photographs (color slides) became my "generative codes," the visual or physical renditions—as in pictures, drawings, stories, articles, films, or other artifacts—of significant themes or problems my students had identified. In class, I projected the images using a Kodak slide projector and we continued to dialogue through Freire's three phases of problem-posing pedagogy.[3] As students viewed the scenes from their neighborhoods and described their lives outside the walls of their confinement, they spoke into a cassette recorder. I transcribed their taped words into typed text and used Roach Van Allen's Language Experience Approach to teach the "word," or basic literacy skills, to the students.[4] We then used Freirean problem-posing pedagogy to critically examine their "world" and further make sense of the injustices they saw and experienced.[5] The students were literally reading their own words to read the world.

Many of us had come to Teacher Corps with experience in home, school, and community activism, and thankfully, we had one another to work through the challenges and opportunities of this first experience in classroom teaching.[6] In retrospect, we were beginning to engage in what Patricia Hill Collins would later call a "rethinking of Black women's activism": "[It] may be more useful to assess Black women's activism less by the ideological content of individual Black women's belief systems—whether they hold conservative, reformist, progressive, or radical ideologies based on some predetermined criteria—and more by Black women's *collective actions* within everyday life that *challenge* domination in these multifaceted domains" [emphasis added].[7]

We were trying to engage in these "collective actions" as teachers serving Black and brown students and trying to "challenge domination" in these "urban correctional" schools. I believe the teachers' narratives in *Teachers of Color: Resisting Racism and Reclaiming Education* embody my own and other teachers' stories. These educators have brought new tools and insights to the individual and collective activist struggle in and out of the classrooms and communities they serve.[8]

There is a history of teachers of Color who have resisted schools' assimilationist goals for students of Color, challenged the deficit framing of students and communities of Color, and disrupted the anti-Black, anti–Mexican American, and racist curriculum in schools.[9] These are teachers who had a set of ethics and values centered on the transformative education of students of Color. They were and are part of a long tradition of transformative educators in the service of racial justice for students, parents, and communities of Color—a service that went unrecognized by the schools they served. We need to recover, document, and honor these stories in our educational history.

In the higher education setting, faculty of Color also speak of this unrecognized labor. It has been referred to as the faculty of Color tax, Black tax, minority tax, and cultural tax. There are at least three dimensions of this tax. First, it is the uncompensated and unrecognized labor (salary or promotion credits) faculty of Color do for the college or university when it comes to dealing with, being a representative for, or serving as an expert on issues of race, equity, and diversity. Second, it is the added stress that race, gender, equity, and diversity work put on the body, mind, and spirit of faculty of Color. Third, it is the added burden that comes with being a person of Color in everyday life—the everyday instances of disrespect and incivility encountered on and off campus.

The tax is also the everyday vigilance it takes to prepare yourself for the world outside your home. It is the reality of working twice as hard to get half as far. And you are not the only one who pays the tax: your family and your community are also taxed. Faculty of Color have been paying this tax and have received little recognition or compensation for their labor. That being said, there is the compensation that salary and promotion can't buy—the joy and value of working with and serving students of Color, colleagues of Color, and communities of Color. The educators of Color in Professor Kohli's book also pay this tax, are impacted by this tax, and—like their higher education colleagues—pay a physical, emotional, and psychological toll.

This book and its powerful counterstories of individual and group activism are an extension of what Professor Kohli started in her dissertation and has been engaging in over the last decade in her subsequent work, of telling the stories of teachers of Color in the K–12 setting. We need more counterstories. We need to recapture the teacher of Color counterstories of our past. We need higher education counterstories. We need to tell more stories of racialization, resistance, and reimagination at all levels. These stories are gifts to this generation of educators and those to follow. At whatever level, these educators pay the tax and still do the work. Because that is who they are: transformative racial justice educators. If they are the dreams, hopes, and aspirations of our ancestral teachers, then what are their dreams, hopes, and aspirations for future generations of educators? Professor Kohli and the counterstories of these thirty transformative educators provide the pathways to answer the question.

I close by congratulating and thanking Rita and the thirty educators in this ground-breaking contribution to the field of education. They have provided us some of the most compelling, asset-based, anti-deficit, anti-sexist, and anti-racist counterstories in K–12 education.

Daniel G. Solórzano
Graduate School of Education and Information Studies
University of California, Los Angeles

1

Introduction

*History and Current Context
for Teachers of Color*

I AM AN EDUCATION PROFESSOR at a minority-serving institution (MSI) in Riverside, California, approximately fifty miles east of Los Angeles. Despite a legacy of the Ku Klux Klan and a large presence of conservative white voters, over the last decade the region has become increasingly diverse as a destination for working-class families of Color fleeing the unaffordable costs of LA housing.[1] Many of the teacher candidates in our teacher education program are from nearby communities, and they are often placed to student teach at schools they or their family members attended.

Rosa, for example, is a Latina in her early twenties who was enrolled in our program and was student teaching at her alma mater, Rubidoux High School (RHS), where 90 percent of students are Latinx, and 81 percent are free or reduced lunch-eligible.[2] One evening in class, I was facilitating a reflection about student teaching experiences and Rosa shared, with tears in her eyes, "I don't belong as a teacher at that school."[3] Her classmate Christina, who was also from the community and placed at the same site, added emotionally, "I feel the same way . . . I'm not sure teaching is the right profession for me."[4] It was devastating to learn that these young women, who had dreams of being transformative educators, did not feel a sense of belonging as teachers within their own community. But how was it that they already felt so defeated at the outset of their careers?

On February 16, 2017, in response to a new US presidency fraught with increasingly emboldened racism and xenophobia, immigrant communities led a national boycott, "A Day Without Immigrants." To demonstrate their importance to the economy, many immigrant families did not go to work, avoided spending money, and kept their children home from school. Numerous students from RHS participated in the strike and did not attend classes that day. In response, one white veteran RHS teacher, Geoffrey Greer, took to social media to voice his perspective:

> Well. A day without immigrants. Perhaps all the missing workers in all the various industries out there had the intended impact and sent the desired message. I don't know. As for the public school system, having my class size reduced by 50% all day long only served to SUPPORT Trump's initiatives and prove how much better things might be without all this overcrowding. . . . That's what you get when you jump on some sort of bandwagon cause as an excuse to be lazy and/or get drunk. Best school day ever.[5]

Mr. Greer was a popular teacher that many students, including Rosa, had looked up to when they were in high school. Yet he publicly made it clear that he had little respect for the lives and resistance efforts of his majority Latinx students or their families. Worse yet, Mr. Greer was not an outlier on the RHS staff. At least five other white teachers from the school responded in support of his stance. Some posted replies such as, "Quieter classes, more productive—let's do this more often," and, "Small classes, trouble makers were gone, fantastic day!"[6]

The community was devastated to learn that they had entrusted their children with teachers who viewed them in such deficit and dehumanizing ways. And these racist ideologies not only were harmful to students and their families, they also led justice-oriented teachers of Color such as Rosa and Christina to doubt their place as educators in their *own* community and the broader profession.

Indeed, racism in schools is nothing new, and neither is its negative impact on diversity in the teaching force. From discriminatory hiring practices to mistreatment by white parents to the deficit ideologies of other teachers, teachers of Color have been made to feel out of place, unwelcomed, or pushed out of public schools.[7] For example, in the years leading up to and after the landmark case of *Brown v. Board of Education of Topeka*, which called for the legal integration of schools, many white parents feared their children would be educated by nonwhite teachers.[8] Across the South, African American principals, teachers, counselors, coaches, band directors, and cafeteria workers—despite their job security or tenure—were harassed, bullied, demoted, and fired.[9] By 1964, 45 percent of Black teachers nationally had unjustly lost their employment.[10] This removal of a critical mass of Black teachers is reflected in today's majority-white teaching force.

In 2020, while students of Color in US public schools make up over 50 percent of the population, teachers of Color constitute just over 20 percent of educators.[11] Based on recent evidence that demonstrates how integral teachers of Color are to the success of students of Color and the educational experiences of all students, the need to diversify the teaching force has become an urgent topic of concern among educational researchers, teacher educators, school leadership, and policy makers alike.[12] As the focus shifts toward recruitment, however, educational stakeholders must still contend with the issue of retention, as teachers of Color leave the profession both sooner and at a higher rate than their white counterparts.[13] And this attrition is often attributed to teachers of Color having debt in a low-paying profession, experiencing poor teaching conditions, and being overrepresented in schools with high staff-turnover rates.[14] Explored less thoroughly is the impact of historical and present-day racism on their professional sustainability.[15] With little change to the structure, policies, and practices of schools, teachers of Color are often being enlisted into spaces that, as we saw with RHS, are racially hostile and detrimental to their well-being.[16]

To understand and address the diversity crisis of the teaching force, it is necessary to move beyond discussions of racial representation. Teachers of Color are not simply vehicles for student success, but rather are whole people with professional goals and oftentimes dreams for their communities. In this book, I invite readers into the lives of thirty justice-oriented teachers of Color to understand the impact of racism in schools on their well-being and their professional retention, growth, and success. Through their narratives, I also explore their resistance to racism and their (re)imagination of classrooms, schools, and districts as they work to reclaim education and create the learning spaces they feel students of Color deserve.

RACISM IN K–12 SCHOOLS

Racism is the creation or maintenance of racial hierarchies supported through institutionalized power.[17] As the governing system of the US was designed, racism was built into laws and policies to

4

protect the wealth and power of those designated as white.[18] The resulting structures have both shaped and justified interpersonal racism (e.g., racial epithets, racial violence) and internalized racism (i.e., beliefs in white cultural superiority) throughout history. And although the overt racism of Jim Crow laws legally ended in 1965, racism continues on, more covertly embedded within the policies, practices, and ideologies that drive institutions—including schools.

Directly tied to racism, *racialization* refers to the processes by which a group of people is prescribed or experiences its racial identity as a means of domination. While various communities of Color in the US have been racialized differently, the process has always worked to uphold whiteness. Thus, while it is important to understand the racism distinct communities have endured, to comprehend the complexity of white supremacy, we must also examine racialization relationally.

For many students of Color, schools have been places of racialization, with forced assimilation to the history, language, and ways of being of dominant communities. Throughout the nineteenth and twentieth centuries, boarding schools and Americanization schools were created to strip Indigenous and Mexican American children of their language and culture.[19] Segregated schools reinforced racial hierarchies of white superiority through the curriculum, limited resources, and unsanitary and unsafe conditions for the education of Black, Native Hawaiian, and Asian American children.[20] Make no mistake: from its historical inception, formal schooling in the US was not designed to serve communities of Color, but rather was created as a place of control and indoctrination.

Unjust practices of K–12 education persist today, as students of Color have disproportionate access to quality, resourced, and

5

culturally sustaining educational opportunities. One-quarter of Black and Latinx students, and almost half of Indigenous students, are denied access to the math and science courses they need to attend a four-year university. Although Black students are 16 percent of the public school student population, Black students constitute 32 percent of in-school suspensions, 46 percent of students with multiple out-of-school suspensions, and 35 percent of school-related arrests.[21] And compared with 13 percent of the general population, over 34 percent of Cambodian, Laotian, and Hmong, and 40 percent of Latinx students, do not graduate high school.[22]

While a myriad of educational policies and practices work in concert to fuel these gross racial disparities, research has demonstrated that the overwhelming whiteness and monolingualism of the teaching profession contributes to the disenfranchisement of students of Color. The current teaching force has been shown to underestimate the abilities of students of Color, to carry deficit beliefs about their families, and to rely on harsh discipline measures or the police.[23] And while teacher racism can be overt, it is also upheld through race-evasive practices.[24] Several studies have featured white teachers who position themselves as "good teachers" but refuse to acknowledge racism and in fact, derailed efforts to disrupt it.[25] A study of fifty-four white teacher candidates on their beliefs about race found that although participants described themselves as "nonbiased" or "far from racist," they continued to engage in negative and accusatory behavior with students of Color that were guided by racializing biases and stereotypes.[26] Since the inception of the schooling system, a predominantly white teaching force has been inextricably linked with the racism communities of Color have suffered.

THE HISTORICAL PRESENCE OF TEACHERS OF COLOR

Throughout this shameful racial history of US public schooling, there have always been teachers of Color who have resisted its assimilationist goals. In addition to education within home, informal, and community settings, teachers of Color have served within formal and government-sponsored school settings to disrupt linguistic and cultural hierarchies and pass along community-based knowledge. Subversive behind school doors, these educators pushed against low expectations, engaged relationally within dehumanizing conditions, and affirmed the worth and agency of students of Color in an unjust world.[27]

For years, Indigenous youth were subjected to government-sponsored boarding schools with the goals of assimilation and cultural annihilation. While these schools were predominantly staffed by white teachers, Indigenous teachers had a presence in their workforce. In 1899, Native Americans composed 45 percent of the Indian School Service, a federal agency responsible for administering government-funded schools: 6 percent served as academic educators and 39 percent were industrial teachers.[28] These Indigenous teachers were seldom seen as capable by white staff *and* were often not trusted in their own communities because of their position in a white educational system. However, some of these teachers resisted strict and culturally violent policies and wove linguistic and cultural affirmation into the curriculum. Tocmetoni Winnemucca, a Paiute author who taught in the Pacific Northwest, and other Indigenous teachers in her context have been described as "trying to preserve Native-American cultural heritage in the face of powerful institutional forces arrayed against it; negotiating with English-only language

7

policies; contending with racist views that remained impervious to even outstanding achievement; [and] struggling with the economic constraints imposed by both gender and race."[29] These teachers endured their own struggles and internal conflicts as they worked simultaneously within and against colonial institutions.

As various racialized groups have been subjected to iterations of assimilationist schooling throughout US history, teachers from the community have acted similarly as disrupters to its goals. In Los Angeles County in the 1920s, when education was guided by overt English-only mandates, the Mexican Consul opened eight schools staffed with Mexican educators who explicitly taught Spanish language and Mexican history. In the 1940s, in response to internment, Japanese-language schools opened for the community to reclaim the education of their youth and instill linguistic and cultural pride.[30] And in the face of dehumanizing policies and practices during segregation, African American teachers engaged the young of their community with support, care, and high expectations.[31]

In her book about an African American school community in the segregated South, Professor Vanessa Siddle Walker complicates the narrative of segregation that focuses only on deplorable conditions and limited resources. To highlight the positive impact of all-Black spaces on young people and their learning, she writes that the "segregated school is most often compared with a 'family' where teachers and principal, with parent-like authority, exercised almost complete autonomy in shaping student learning."[32] Siddle Walker goes on to share that many Black families were actually interested in maintaining segregated schools because in these Black contexts, they were respected and valued, as school attended to their children's holistic needs.

Feminist author bell hooks affirms Siddle Walker's description of segregated schools based on her own education.[33] hooks argues that despite material limitations, schools were a place where Black teachers were committed to the academic success of Black students and there was support and encouragement to excel. Thus, when desegregation was mandated and seen by many as a victory for Black, Latinx, and Asian American students who would have better access to the academic and economic opportunities of whites, numerous Black families lamented the transition. Left with few Black teachers and little community control of education, many Black students lost a support system of people who cared deeply about their culturally sustained learning. hooks shares:

> School changed utterly with racial integration. Gone was the messianic zeal to transform our minds and beings that had characterized teachers and their pedagogical practices in our all-black schools. Knowledge was suddenly about information only. It had no relation to how one lived, behaved. It was no longer connected to antiracist struggle . . . . Now, we were mainly taught by white teachers whose lessons reinforced racist stereotypes. For black children, education was no longer about the practice of freedom.[34]

As hooks explains, an impassioned investment in the learning of Black students was lost through integration. Although Black students now had access to more functional facilities and resources, they no longer went to schools with Black educators who cared about them or their shared struggles for liberation. Instead, white teachers became a mechanism to reinforce racist ideologies of Black intellectual deficiencies.

As desegregation efforts spread, schools engaged in policies such as rezoning and tracking to maintain racial divisions and preserve hierarchies. By the 1960s, the civil rights movement emerged as a response to continued inequitable and unjust social conditions. Communities of Color were demanding rights and respect, and education was a vital part of this platform. Within this activism materialized both a multiracial movement of ethnic studies and Freedom Schools, educational spaces organized by Black communities to expose students to Black history, literature, and resistance.[35] As student activism soared, one of the common demands was to increase teachers of Color. For example, in 1968, Chicanx students from the Los Angeles Unified School District organized against the unjust and culturally neglectful conditions of their schools in a series of protests known as the East Los Angeles Walkouts. In addition to demands for culturally sustaining curriculum, better resources, and increased college access, students and community organizers cited the need for more teachers from the community—where 23 percent of students but only 3 percent of teachers were Chicanx. Building upon this foundation, California State University, Northridge started Operation Chicano Teacher in 1973 to recruit and provide academic support to activist-oriented Latinx students interested in education careers.[36]

THE CURRENT CONTEXT OF TEACHERS OF COLOR

With attention on the glaring racial disparities of academic access within public schools and the lack of diversity in the teaching force, pressure to address "minority teacher shortages" began to mount in the 1980s and 1990s. Scholars and activists began pointing to racism and xenophobia within hiring practices, and called for recruitment strategies to grow the presence of teachers of Color.[37] Since then, research has supported these demands by demonstrating how teachers of Color academically and social-emotionally engage students of Color: they are more likely to have cultural match, serve as cultural brokers with the community, and see students of Color as capable learners.[38] Additionally, teachers of Color have been shown to have insight into the racialized experiences of students of Color and stand as their supports and advocates.[39] For example, studies found that Latinx youth believed teachers of Color had higher confidence in student abilities and cared for them like family.[40] In North Carolina, another study found that Black students who have a Black teacher are significantly less likely to be removed from classrooms or schools as punishment.[41]

Even as the numbers of students of Color in US public schools are steadily increasing, teachers of Color continue to be underrepresented and also leave the profession at a disproportionate rate. In the 2017–2018 school year, although just 48 percent of public schools nationally were made up of white students, 79 percent of teachers were white. And while Indigenous teachers comprised just 1 percent of both students and teachers within public schools, Asian American Pacific Islander (AAPI), Black, and Latinx students made up 6 percent, 15 percent, and 27 percent of the population, respectively, yet AAPI teachers constituted under 3 percent, Black teachers constituted 7 percent, and Latinx teachers were just 9 percent of the educator workforce (see figure 1.1).[42]

As a response, there has been an uptick in recruitment efforts, including scholarships for underrepresented teachers and "homegrown" programs where college students of Color, paraprofessionals, or community workers are supported to become classroom teachers in their own communities.[43] Some initiatives start recruitment even earlier, partnering with local high schools to track students of Color toward the teaching force.[44] While these programs are doing significant work to change the demographics

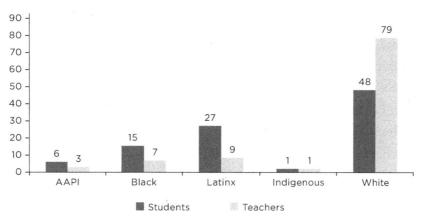

FIGURE 1.1 US public school student and teacher demographics

of their local teaching force, homegrown models are neither wide-spread nor typically designed to confront racism on a structural or systemic level.

And so, despite current efforts to increase the number of teachers of Color, their marginalization persists across the teaching pipeline. In teacher education programs, where the majority of teacher candidates and teacher educators are white, curriculum and pedagogy tends to neglect the experiences and perspectives of teachers of Color.[45] Teachers of Color in these spaces have articulated neglect of their visions for the profession and reported feeling invisible, silenced, and isolated.[46] In the field, moreover, they have attested to experiencing *racial microaggressions* (small but significant, everyday racial assaults), being forced to serve as racial experts, being stereotyped and limited to particular professional roles, and feeling triggered as they witness students experience racism that they themselves endured in their own education.[47] Teachers of Color have additionally shared that their community-oriented visions of education are in direct contradiction to the individualizing and competitive structure of schools, and they often feel like outliers to the culture of their campuses and the profession at large.[48]

CRITICAL RACE THEORY

Teachers of Color offer a great deal in realizing a rigorous, culturally sustaining, and humanizing education for students of Color, but racism persistently impedes these efforts. As we diversify the teaching force, there must be a deeper understanding of the racialization teachers of Color experience professionally and a stronger intention to recognize them as complex people that endure harm and who are capable of leading transformation. In this book, I use the lens of critical race theory (CRT) to analyze narratives of teachers of Color, identifying racism in the professional policies and practices of K–12 schools and exploring the power of resistance and reimagination in reclaiming the education of communities of Color.

Originally a legal theory, CRT was designed to challenge race-evasive and meritocratic explanations for racial inequity that blamed communities of Color for their subordinate social and economic positions. Scholars Daniel Solórzano, Gloria Ladson-Billings, and William Tate brought CRT into the landscape of educational scholarship in the late 1990s to draw attention to institutional racism as the root of racial disparities in education.[49] Solórzano began by asking questions such as, "What forms does racism take in teacher education and how are these forms used to maintain the subordination of students of Color?"[50] And Ladson-Billings built from CRT to argue "that the historical, economic, sociopolitical, and moral decisions and policies that characterize our society have created an education debt" owed to Black, Indigenous, and students of Color.[51]

Over the last two decades, the impact of CRT in education has grown tremendously, drawing attention to institutional racism in schools, with particular focus on student experiences.[52] Yet limited attention has been paid to teachers of Color who exist in the same racializing contexts. Throughout the chapters of this book, I utilize CRT and its related concepts to unpack the complexity of racism and racial justice in the experiences of teachers of Color—from their own K–12 education to their positions as K–12 educators. By analyzing narratives diverse in terms of race, ethnicity, age, class, gender and sexuality, and geography, I offer a nuanced and intersectional analysis of racism in schools and reveal the racializing structural forces that marginalize teachers of Color. Additionally, in the tradition of CRT's focus on the power and possibility of communities of Color, I have structured this book to display the strength and agency of teachers of Color committed to justice as they resist messages that they do not belong, and reimagine schools as a place where they and their students can thrive.[53]

TEACHER OF COLOR COUNTERSTORIES

I am a second-generation immigrant, South Asian woman who began my career in education as a middle school special education teacher, where I served working-class students of Color who were labeled with disabilities. For many years now, I have worked as a teacher educator and educational researcher of issues of race and racism in schools. I have also collaborated to develop and facilitate spaces that foster the racial justice leadership development and activism of teachers of Color. Additionally, I am a parent of elementary-aged children who, like all young people, deserve teachers that reflect them, respect their positionalities, and center their ways of knowing. It is from all these layers of my personal and professional experiences that I write this book.

The theoretical frames, data, and analyses I present are rooted in over a decade of research where I have explored the experiences of justice-oriented teachers of Color at different stages of their trajectories toward and within teaching. I have completed interviews and focus groups with teacher candidates of Color enrolled in teacher education programs who reflected on the role of race and racism across their K–16 academic journeys.[54] I have also engaged in research focused on the racialized experiences of practicing teachers of Color, which included over five hundred qualitative questionnaire responses and more than fifty digital narratives and interviews.[55] I have additionally conducted formal and informal interviews with veteran educators of Color to explore their leadership roles in racial justice initiatives within their schools or districts.[56] For this book, I pair the data and findings from each of those studies with new in-depth interviews to present thirty narratives of Black, Latinx, Asian American, and Pacific Islander K–12 public school teachers who work in schools serving primarily students of Color, and who are committed to issues of social and racial justice.[57] The teachers span from preservice to veteran educators, and are diverse in positionality (see table 1.1 for more details). Their unique stories collectively reveal important truths about racism in our educational system and the powerful resistance that teachers of Color employ throughout their academic and professional journeys.

I relay the accounts of teachers of Color guided by the CRT-informed method of counterstorytelling. In contrast to a *majoritarian story*—a narrative commonly accepted as truth and told from the vantage point of the powerful—a *counterstory* is told from the perspective of marginalized people as a means to challenge power,

TABLE 1.1   Teacher participants

Name	Race/ethnicity[a]
Alberto	Latino
Amanda	African American
Andrea	Puerto Rican
Bayani	Pilipino
Carla	Latina
Christina	Korean American
Darnell	African American
Elaine	Korean American
Elena	Chicana
Emiko	Asian American: Japanese and Irish
Erin	Biracial Black
Eva	Afro-Latina, Dominican
Gloria	Chicana
Imani	Black: Ugandan and Belizean
Jeffrey	African American
Jennifer	Latina
Joaquin	Latinx
Julia	Nicaraguan
Julian	Chicano
Karrie	African American and Puerto Rican
Lamar	African American
Lelei	Samoan
Leticia	Latina
Liza	Chicana
Mateo	Mexican
Maya	African American
Rachel	Biracial Black
Ramona	Mexican American
Salina	Black
Sonali	South Asian

[a] The race/ethnicity included for participants represents their self-designation.

[b] The regions are as specific or general as participants wanted to protect their anonymity.

Position	Region[b]
High school world history teacher	Los Angeles, California
High school science teacher	Los Angeles, California
Elementary school teacher	Brooklyn, New York
High school English and social studies teacher	Stockton, California
Elementary school teacher	Coachella Valley, California
High school English teacher	Los Angeles, California
High school math teacher	San Francisco Bay Area, California
High school English teacher	Decatur, Georgia
High school English teacher	South Los Angeles, California
Elementary school teacher	San Francisco Bay Area, California
High school English teacher	Omaha, Nebraska
High school English teacher	Bronx, New York
Elementary school teacher	Southern California
Middle school history teacher	South Los Angeles, California
High school Spanish teacher	San Francisco Bay Area, California
Elementary school teacher	East Los Angeles, California
Middle school social studies teacher	Sacramento, California
Elementary school teacher	Southern California
High school English teacher	Coachella, California
High school history teacher	Los Angeles, California
Elementary school teacher	Fairfax, Virginia
Elementary school teacher	Oʻahu, Hawaiʻi
Elementary school teacher	Southern California
Bilingual high school English teacher	San Francisco Bay Area, California
High school math teacher	Eastern Washington
High school social studies teacher	New York City, New York
High school English teacher	Minneapolis, Minnesota
Elementary school teacher	Suburb of Saint Paul, Minnesota
Middle school science teacher	Southern California
High school math teacher	Pacific Northwest

reframe deficit myths, and reveal structures and practices that contribute to inequity.[58] Milner and Howard argue that a counterstory "provides space for researchers to reinterpret, disrupt or to interrupt pervasive discourses that may paint communities and people, particularly communities and people of color, in grim, dismal ways."[59] In this book, the counterstories serve to challenge the normalcy of an overwhelmingly white teaching force and highlight institutional policies and practices that function to sideline teachers of Color. Specifically, I aim to (a) disrupt complacency around the high rates of teacher of Color attrition, (b) interrogate the role of racism and racial climate in their pushout, and (c) center the assets teachers of Color bring to the classroom as they resist the current context and radically transform schools. I construct these counterstories by weaving together direct quotes and narrative descriptions of the experiences of teacher participants with critical research and analyses of racism. The teachers have also provided input on the written narratives to ensure their experiences and understandings have been authentically captured.

LANGUAGE AND LABELS

Throughout this book, I use labels to describe people. I want to first acknowledge that labels for race, ethnicity, or other social groupings are constructed, are politically influenced, and change over time. While many of these categories were created as tools to oppress, racialized people have also reclaimed labels, pridefully embracing the community and collective agency built within these terms.[60] Thus, it is important for me to take care as I operationalize and use them.

The first term to explain is at the center of this book: teachers of Color. The concept "of Color" has been used frequently to aggregate various groups of racially minoritized people, centering their shared experiences as racialized in a society dominated by whiteness. People have at times contested this concept for the ways it essentializes or collapses the experiences and needs of individual racialized groups, particularly the unique histories, experiences, and trauma of Black and Indigenous peoples.[61]

In this book, I use the racial identifiers that participants chose for themselves within their counterstories, and I build upon scholarship that centers those specific racialized communities (e.g., Black, Indigenous, Latinx, Asian American). I use the term *teachers of Color* when speaking of racialized teachers in the aggregate. I do so with recognition of its flaws and limitations in representing the nuanced positionalities of diverse people within and across racial and ethnic lines, and with the understanding that white supremacy, settler colonialism, and antiblackness are intimately related and have shaped dynamics of harm between and among racialized people. I fully acknowledge that a Black man who is an elementary school teacher in Virginia has fundamentally different sociopolitical, racial, and gendered experiences than a South Asian woman math teacher from the Pacific Northwest, *and* I argue there is a utility in reading diverse stories of racialization side-by-side, as it sharpens our understanding of how racism operates to maintain the social order. Because the narratives of this book are from a diverse range of Black, Latinx, Asian American, and Pacific Islander teachers who see their own struggles as interrelated, I use the term *teachers of Color* also to recognize the solidarity they foster as they work to resist and reclaim schools.

The next label I want to define is *Black*. I employ this term throughout the book to describe people of African descent from around the world—including African Americans, as well as people from African nations, the Caribbean, and Latin America.

Additionally, I seek to clarify my use of the label *Latinx*. I am aware that, precisely through the powerful organizing and activism of women, the longstanding labels of *Chicano* and *Latino* were challenged and transformed to *Chicana/o* and *Latina/o*, and that many historians, scholars, activists, and others recognize the legacy of their struggle against patriarchy represented in those terms. It is upon that foundation of activism for inclusion that new generations of Latinx activists have pushed past the gender binary of the *a/o* toward a term that is inclusive of gender-nonconforming members of the community. I use the term *Latinx* not to erase the important activism of women who have fought for their visibility, but instead to stand with those in the Latinx community who have built upon the legacies of powerful Chicanas and Latinas to strive for intersectional visibility and justice.[62]

BOOK STRUCTURE

The book is divided into three main themes: racialization (chapters 2 and 3), resistance (chapter 4), and reimagination (chapter 5). The racialization chapters examine both the racism that teachers of Color experience and the impact of that racism. Chapter 2 includes a series of counterstories of teachers of Color in their journeys to and in the classroom, with a specific focus on their experiences with racism. The chapter explores (a) narratives about how peers, teachers, and administrators contributed to or were complicit in the hostile racial climates that teachers of Color experienced as K–12 students; (b) descriptions by teacher candidates of Color about how peers, the curriculum, faculty supervisors, and guiding teachers served to marginalize them as they worked toward becoming educators; and (c) examples of critical teachers of Color—novice and veteran alike—describing ways in which other teachers and school administrators racialized them by questioning their pedagogy, ignoring their insights, and overlooking them for leadership opportunities.

Extending chapter 2's descriptions of the racism teachers of Color endure, in chapter 3 I describe the impact of racism on them professionally and personally through experiences with racial stress, racial battle fatigue, and their racialized pushout from schools. The narratives show the toll that layers of institutional and interpersonal racism in teacher education and teaching have on teachers of Color, diminishing their professional self-efficacy and exacerbating isolation, anxiety, and depression. The counterstories also reveal how hostile racial climates cause teachers of Color to leave their schools or contemplate leaving the profession.

Next, the book explores the survival and resistance of teachers of Color. Chapter 4 identifies three tools teachers of Color utilize to navigate the hostile racial climates they are experiencing: their racial literacies, developing communities of resistance, and organizing for change. Many of the teachers in the data described their family members or past teachers as sources of critical analyses of schooling when they were young, and they discuss how these experiences provided them resilience against racism and served as the foundation to their resistance and vision for transformative schooling. The teachers also identify the importance of critical professional development (CPD)—professional development spaces that support the political orientations and critical pedagogical needs of justice-oriented teachers. Across various contexts in their lives, teachers of Color strengthened their racial literacies, built communities, and organized in institutionalized and grassroots ways, developing into the educators and activists they wished to be. In this chapter I portray the assets teachers of Color bring to the profession and how they use their power and agency to resist policies and practices that exacerbate racial inequity.

From forcible acculturation to inadequate resources, schools function in oppressive ways for students of Color. Although school change is often framed as being in the hands of school administrators and state and federal policy makers, teachers of Color have led powerful initiatives to transform the educational experiences of students of Color. Starting from the notion of a radical imagination—a means to visualize and move toward a society where humanity, joy, and possibility is central for communities of Color—chapter 5 moves past a stance of opposition to a place of dreaming.[63] This chapter includes counterstories of teachers who conceived and led efforts to reclaim classrooms, schools, and districts as engaged, culturally and community sustaining sites of learning. These narratives include restorative science pedagogy, an education centered on the land and legacies of students' ancestors, youth research where students of Color have collaborated to lead tangible change in their communities, and the development of a districtwide ethnic studies initiative where the hiring practices, professional development, and the teaching of all academic disciplines were reconceptualized to center the experiences and needs of the community. Ultimately, the chapter affirms the possibilities of educational transformation in the hands of critical teachers of Color.

Chapter 6 concludes the book by offering a summative analysis of the collective narratives. I describe the implications of hostile racial climates on the overall diversity of the US teaching force and synthesize a description of the assets and power teachers of Color bring into the profession. This chapter also provides concrete suggestions on what teacher education programs and K–12 schools can do to better support the well-being of teachers of Color, and it reminds teachers of Color of their power and their deserved place in schools.

Throughout this book, the narratives of teachers of Color are often deeply personal and emotionally charged. They have shared vulnerably, and I take great care as I write to honor their struggles, their resistance, and the profound hope and promise they provide.

2

"I am being perceived as a threat"

The Racialization of Teachers of Color

FOURTEEN-YEAR-OLD Muslim freshman Ahmed Mohamed was well known among his high school classmates as "Inventor Kid" for his advanced skills with engineering and electronics. In September 2015, Ahmed brought a homemade clock to his Irving, Texas, high school to show his engineering teacher. But his English teacher, who Ahmed saw first that morning, thought it was a bomb and reported it to the school principal, who then alerted the police. Within a few hours, Ahmed was questioned, handcuffed, and transported to a juvenile detention center; he had been accused of purposely causing a bomb scare. Although he continued to assert throughout the incident that he had made a clock and not a bomb, district officials and the state governor all expressed their support for the actions of the school.[1]

Bayan Zehlif was a hijab-wearing Muslim high school student from Rancho Cucamonga, California. Attending school with a peer that tweeted, "All Muslims are terrorists," and with a teacher who argued in class, "The people who caused 9/11 shouldn't be here today," in May 2016 Bayan learned that her own year-book picture had been labeled "Isis Phillips." She later posted on Facebook that school administrators had reached out to her and claimed that it was a typo.[2] Fearful of being the target of more hate, she left the school for the last weeks of her senior year, returning only for exams.

In November 2017, a Muslim student from Lake Braddock Secondary School in Fairfax County, Virginia, had her hijab "ripped from her head" by a male teacher, who then said, "Oh, your hair is so pretty!" This teacher later claimed he thought he was pulling off her hoodie. The teacher was placed on leave by the school district, but students at the school then began harassing and cyberbullying their classmate for reporting the popular educator.[3]

In very different contexts, these three Muslim children all experienced acts of racializing fear, hate, and disrespect from their peers and teachers. Equally concerning was the response from school leadership who did little (if anything) to ensure Muslim students' safety or inclusion. Although they belong to a religion that spans racial categories, Black and brown Muslim communities in the United States have been racialized throughout time. From denials of Arab citizenship in the early twentieth century to George W. Bush's post–September 11 "War on Terror" to Donald Trump's Executive Order 13769 (commonly referred to as the "Muslim ban") and his use of anti-Muslim rhetoric throughout his 2016 and 2020 presidential campaigns, Islamophobia has had a firm place in the historical, institutional, legal, and ideological fabric of the United States. And while crimes against Muslims had been on the rise—up 67 percent in 2015, another 27 percent in 2016—in the first ten days of the Trump administration, 37 percent of reported harassment of Muslim Americans had occurred within educational institutions. In a report by the Southern Poverty Law Center issued six months after the presidential election, one-third of K–12 teachers across the US reported an increase in anti-immigrant and anti-Muslim sentiments used against students, including harassment, threats, and epithets such as "terrorist," "ISIS," and "bomber."[4]

Like all children, Muslim students should be able to attend schools where they feel safe, respected, and even celebrated. But how can that happen when the very people relied upon to care for them do not recognize the terrorizing racism embedded in policies, practices, or ideologies within the school? A proposed solution has been to diversify the educator force. Research suggests that if schools hire more teachers that reflect the race, cultures, and languages of the increasingly diverse student population, then schools would have a stronger capacity to teach in culturally sustaining ways and would be better equipped to identify, address, or prevent racism. For example, African American students who had at least one African American teacher in their elementary years had significantly higher reading scores than those with no African American teachers, and, as I mentioned in chapter 1, were disciplined far less harshly.[5] And while not all teachers have the capacity or will, studies have also demonstrated that teachers of Color tend to be more oriented to resist injustice and advocate for and with students of Color.[6]

However, despite the benefits that teachers of Color bring into schools, diversification alone cannot solve racism. If administrators and policy makers do not address the racial hierarchies that schools were designed around or do not rewrite policies and practices that uphold racial injustice, teachers of Color will continue being recruited into and subjected to the same hostile racial climates students experience. Take as one example Maimona

Afzal Berta, a hijab-wearing middle school teacher from San Jose, California. Throughout 2017, there were at least fifteen reported anti-Muslim incidents from students at her school, including derogatory comments and threatening gestures to her and a hijab-wearing classroom aide and afterschool supervisor. On September 11 that year, she got to school early, excited to start *Harry Potter and the Sorcerer's Stone* with her students. When she entered her classroom, however, she found it defaced with anti-Muslim slurs. In an interview with the *Mercury News*, Berta confided, "It was devastating. I felt completely targeted, and not even safe in a place I consider home." While Berta's presence as a teacher may have affirmed the identities or belongingness of Muslim or other minoritized students, there was nothing in place to protect *her* from racism embedded in the culture and climate of the school.[7]

Teachers of Color have been navigating the racial climates of schools since they were students and continue to confront racism in their professional lives. To sustain a diverse teaching force, teacher education programs, schools, and districts must first acknowledge the entrenched systems of oppression that make school a hostile place for people of Color—students and educators alike. In this chapter, I include counterstories of teachers of Color who carry goals of transforming schools for communities of Color yet have endured racism within their K–12 education, within their teacher education, and in their role as teachers. As their narratives unfold, you will hear complexity and tension in their experiences. Although they share a commitment to justice, there is great diversity in their positionalities—being from different regions, urban or rural settings, and elementary or secondary schools, and varying in their race, gender, class, and culture. And yet there is a haunting ubiquity to the racism they describe in schools as they endure the hardships of being people of Color and fighting for and with students of Color in schools that center and affirm whiteness.

K-12 SCHOOLING

The racism that students of Color experience has been documented over time, and as I shared in chapter 1, manifests in many ways, including resource allocation, hierarchies of knowledge, deficit thinking, and discipline. Less attention has been spent unpacking what it means when teachers have experienced racism in their own K–12 education. While teacher preparation programs strive to provide new and responsive ways to engage students in their learning, much of a teacher's professional knowledge is shaped by more than a decade of experiences attending school. And since so many teachers of Color have had their own histories, languages, phenotype, culture, and ways of being and knowing demeaned and devalued, they also have to unlearn and resist the dominant structures that question their place in school. Here I present counterstories of three critical teachers of Color who are working hard to create engaging and transformative educational opportunities for young people while carrying traumatic memories of how school rejected their cultural wealth and that of their families and communities. Abby is an African American high school science teacher, Elaine is a Korean American high school English teacher, and Jennifer is a Latina fifth-grade teacher. The narratives of their K–12 education reveal how the structures and policies of schools intertwine with the actions of students and teachers to construct a hostile racial climate where, as young people, they could not thrive as their full selves.

Abby: The Cumulative Injury of Racial Microaggressions

Abby is an African American high school science teacher in Southern California. Teaching relevant units on food justice and sexual health, she is beloved by the students in the working-class, Black and Latinx community in which she teaches. Her critical and justice-oriented commitments to her students were shaped by racism she experienced within her own educational history.

Abby's mother, Sylvia, started her career as a teacher in a predominantly Black community in Oakland, California, where she was born and where she had Abby. After splitting up with Abby's father, Sylvia found a higher-paying job teaching in a predominantly white suburb, so she decided to move and enroll her daughter in school there. For the rest of elementary school, Abby was the only Black student in her classes and in afterschool care.

Abby remembers being called the *n*-word often at school—when a peer did not want to sit next to her, for example, or if she had a conflict with another student. She even remembers one day being called the *n*-word for winning a game of tetherball during recess—the boy got angry and embarrassed for losing the game, so he asserted the racial power he had over her. Since the mostly white teachers at the school had done very little to address the racist language that was frequently hurled at her, that day Abby finally told her mother. Sylvia was furious, but as one of the only Black women on staff in a school permissive of racism, advocating for her daughter proved futile—in the end, nothing was done.

When Abby got to middle and high school, her environment was more diverse. She was no longer the only Black student at school, yet the racialization continued. As opposed to the overt slurs of her elementary years, the new racism she experienced included racial microaggressions—micro, covert, conscious, or unconscious manifestations of racism that reinforce racial stratification and cumulatively take a toll.[8] Often disguised as compliments or jokes, the racial microaggressions Abby experienced worked to uphold racial hierarchies of white racial and cultural superiority. Abby's peers would differentiate her from the majority of Black students at the school, saying, "You're a cool Black person," "You're a white-Black girl," or, "You know, you're a proper Black person." But these apparent "compliments" were actually forms of antiblack racism, as they evaluated Abby's worth relative to whiteness and pitted her against her community.[9]

As racism operates, however, her white peers' perception that Abby was different or better than other Black students did not serve to protect her from the pervasive harm of antiblackness. Abby recalls that her predominantly white teachers were repeatedly surprised by her intellectual ability—they never called on her in class, and they often assumed she had not turned in her work. She explained: "They always tried to categorize me, or assume I wasn't going to do my work or be efficient. And I think a lot of times I fell into their thought and was very ineffective. The low expectations ended up having a deep effect on me and I ended up doing poorly in classes that I knew the material."

The racism that Abby experienced from her elementary through high school years was both overt and veiled, at times cloaked as "compliments." Yet despite its form, it was inescapable—woven into the culture and climate of her schooling. And all of these experiences took a toll on her; not only did Abby's grades suffer, but the racism she experienced impacted her engagement with school and her self-perception.

Elaine: When Teachers Condone Racial Harm

Born in Georgia to Korean immigrant parents, Elaine is a high school English teacher. She grew up in Decatur, a city northeast of Atlanta, and was the only student of Korean descent in schools with primarily African American and Latinx students and some Cambodian students. Having little interaction with other Korean kids, Elaine connected to cultural aspects of her Black and Latinx classmates, yet she was not fully embraced by her peers or supported by her teachers.

Elaine had many negative experiences in school where she was teased for her language and appearance. She recalls students pulling their eyes and calling her "chinita," or saying "ching, chong, ching, chong" to her often. A group of harassing students called themselves "chink-patrol," but as with Abby, when Elaine would tell teachers, they were typically unresponsive. Elaine elaborated: "I have really bad memories of teachers being like, 'I can't do anything about it, sorry.' You know, where you just feel really powerless. Your first instinct is to retaliate, but I was patient and went and told the teacher, but I got no response from her. I felt stupid, like I was just being a tattletale, because in the end there was no kind of punishment or consequence for the other person." While Elaine's teachers were not the perpetrators of racist remarks, they were responsible for the climate of their classrooms and of the school. Not only did teachers never validate Elaine's linguistic or cultural identity, but their lack of intervention when her peers mocked her left her feeling isolated and believing that racism was acceptable in school. These repeated and cumulative experiences also made Elaine feel ashamed of her language and family. She shared, "My mom isn't a soft-spoken lady; she has a very loud voice and a lot of times when she was speaking in Korean, I would be embarrassed in public because I felt like people would think, 'Oh, Asian languages sound like all 'ching-chong-chong.'"[10] The aggregate of racism Elaine faced in school caused her to internalize inferiority, and she began to believe that her mother was contributing to the problem when she spoke in Korean. In turn, Elaine stopped speaking in her native language through the rest of her K–12 education. She only began to reclaim it after college when she studied the language and then moved to Korea to teach English.

Jennifer: Deficit Thinking and the Withholding of a Quality Education

Jennifer is a Latina fifth-grade teacher in the Los Angeles area, serving students who are 100 percent Latinx and mostly Spanish-speaking. Dedicated to engaging her students in meaningful and culturally sustaining education, she wants them to grow up with a strong sense of cultural and linguistic pride that she herself had been denied within her schooling. She plans units that explore and validate students' migration stories, and creates sustained relationships with their families that acknowledges and builds upon their assets.

Jennifer grew up in a similar working-class Latinx community about twenty-five miles east of Los Angeles, where most residents worked in nearby factories, in construction, or as gardeners. Although Jennifer was born in California and had US citizenship, she grew up with undocumented family members and carried great stress throughout her childhood from the threat of loved ones being deported. While Jennifer's parents did not go to college and could not always help her navigate the process, they always stressed that higher education was important and supported her academic journey.

Throughout her K–12 schooling most of Jennifer's teachers were white, very few reflected her culture or language in their curriculum or pedagogy, and many had low expectations of the students—not providing structured or engaging lessons, and then not caring if they skipped class. In high school, Jennifer recalls teachers and counselors projecting intersectionally racist and sexist stereotypes onto her peers, telling girls that they would not finish school because they were just going to get pregnant, and belittling young women like Jennifer who had aspirations for higher education.

When Jennifer did graduate, she went on to community college. It was in that new space that she realized how underprepared she was. She struggled to catch up in her writing and other academic skills, but she persisted and ended up transferring to an elite four-year university. She did not, however, shake the way her education had continually deemed her community unworthy of learning. Aware of differences in her foundational training, Jennifer was hesitant to speak in class or ask questions when she did not understand, afraid she would confirm to others the idea that she was incapable.

Jennifer's parents were invested in her education and cared about her success, but the educators in her community who believed that Latinx families do not value education or that Latinx students do not have the capacity to succeed served as an immense barrier to academic attainment for her and many others. Education scholar Richard Valencia has argued that these deficit cultural myths are steeped in legacies of racist pseudoscience that (a) have historically been used to justify tracking Latinx students into manual labor, and (b) continue to linguistically and culturally alienate students and their families from engagement.[11] Today, for every one hundred Latinx students that enter elementary school, an average of just twelve students complete four-year college degrees, which is less than half the number of white students and less than one-third the number of Asian American students graduating.[12] When we consider the low number of Latinx educators in public schools, Jennifer's narrative allows us to see how the alienating culture and hostile racial climate of K–12 schools contribute to this cycle.

Abby, in a predominantly white setting; Erika, in a community of Color that did not reflect her identity; and Jennifer, in a city of shared language and culture, all struggled in their education because of racialized stereotypes from peers and/or teachers that negatively shaped their self-perceptions, self-efficacy, and opportunities. Where many do not, however, these women of Color had advocates in their lives that affirmed their educational capabilities and worth. Despite the harm they endured, they were able to graduate and eventually access higher education, which included opportunities such as ethnic studies, heritage Study Abroad programs, and campus cultural organizations that helped them to heal and reclaim the value of their languages, cultures, and communities.

TEACHER EDUCATION

Even for those who had healing experiences in their undergraduate education, students of Color who pursue teaching often continue their racialized struggles in their teacher preparation. As recent reports show, 70 percent of students, 87 percent of adjunct instructors, and 91 percent of tenured/tenure-track instructors in teacher education programs are white.[13] Additionally, as teacher education is often reduced to a technical profession, predominantly white cohorts of teacher candidates seldom encounter theories that expose systems of oppression.[14] Instead, the resulting environment transmits and reproduces policies and practices that result in racialized harm for teacher candidates of Color and students of Color in K–12 schools.[15] I share the counternarratives of four teacher candidates of Color in two teacher education contexts, both with an explicitly social justice mission: Maya, a Black woman in an elite, private, predominantly white university in New York City; and Julia, Gloria, and Leticia, three Latinas enrolled in a large, public minority-serving institution (MSI)–designated university in Southern California.

Maya: Black Alienation in a Predominantly White Institution

Her mother a nurse and her father a physician, Maya was born and raised in an upper-middle-class and predominantly white suburb of Richmond, Virginia. Attending honors classes as one of three African American girls in the magnet program was a challenging and racializing experience. Similar to what Abby described about her schooling, peers would tell Maya, "You are so articulate," or "You are not like those other Black girls." They focused a lot on her Blackness and would often joke about her permed hair when she would not go swimming. Being her whole self in this space was challenging, and Maya experienced anxiety throughout her social sphere.

When she arrived at a top-tier public college in her state, many of her classmates diminished her accomplishments with unfounded claims that her acceptance was simply due to affirmative action. Seeking supportive spaces, Maya decided to double major in history and African diasporic studies. In classes that were majority Black with mostly Black professors, Maya said for the first time she felt free. She reflected:

> History helped me with my personal journey of understanding and accepting myself and loving myself; understanding where race comes from societally and personally. I wanted to get into education because I had learned so much about my own experiences. Recognizing that I was harmed in my prior experiences, I wanted to be the person that would help mitigate that for other people. To make sure that high schoolers don't have the same experience I had—that they are getting the stuff that they need, that I didn't get until I was twenty.

It was through critical history that Maya began to make sense of her experiences and was now able to love her hair, her skin, and her people. And with this love, she decided to become a teacher, to provide Black students and other students of Color the (healing) historical perspective she was never given as a young person.

As she began to think about graduate school, a professor helped her apply and secure a scholarship to a prestigious college in New York City with a social justice mission. Maya was excited for the opportunity to learn to teach in a large urban district with a significant Black population like New York City Public Schools, but when she got there from the liberatory Black space of her undergraduate education, it was jarring to find out she was the only Black student in the social studies credential program. Aside from Maya, one Latina from the Bronx, and one Asian American man, the teacher candidates were all white and wealthy.

Also new to the city, Maya felt isolated in this space. There was no one to process her journey as a suburban Black educator in urban schools, and when she challenged her peers' limited understanding about topics such as inequity, race, and segregation, there was no one to back her up or to commiserate with. The anxiety of Maya's K–12 education seeped back in as she sat through classes where she shouldered the burden of being *the* Black voice in class. She shared the exhausting toll of this racism:

> I really had to choose my words carefully. I was always thinking about what I was going to say, making sure that it could be fact-checked. Especially if we were in a discussion, I would have to be really conscious of what I was doing, how I was speaking, and what I was saying. If I said something, I would overthink, "Was that something I should have said?" I was really cognizant of how people were going to respond to it. The work I had to put in to make a point! I was just really conscious of myself in the space, of being the only one.

Watching her privileged classmates be "spoon-fed" knowledge about inequity and injustice that was obvious to her but that they had never considered, she realized that she was "enrolled in a program designed to teach white people how to interact with people of Color." Maya was neither challenged nor engaged in discourse that was going to move her toward her vision of being a critical Black educator for her community. Learning to be a teacher is intense and overwhelming for anyone, but the racism Maya experienced in a program claiming to serve Black and brown students of New York City schools made her program a "hard time that she was just going to get through."

Sadly, Maya's experience is not unique. Research has repeatedly confirmed that predominantly white institutions (PWIs) have been hostile spaces for teacher candidates of Color. Faced with white teacher candidates' deficit views of communities of Color and resistance to discussing race, teacher educators' avoidance of critical issues, and a curriculum geared toward white teachers, teachers of Color in these spaces often feel marginalized, "othered," and that they do not belong in the profession.[16] In Maya's case, it was in this liberal white space where she felt both invisible and hypervisible in her positionality as a Black teacher candidate.

Julia, Gloria, and Leticia: Centering Whiteness in a Minority-Serving Institution

With a longstanding documentation of the overwhelming whiteness of teacher education, the shifting teaching demographics of PWIs comes with many challenges.[17] Recent scholars and policy makers have pointed to MSIs as an undervalued space in the development of teachers of Color. As historically Black colleges and universities (HBCUs); tribal colleges; Hispanic-serving institutions (HSIs); and Asian American, Native American, and Pacific Islander–serving institutions (AANAPISI) are already enrolling a majority of students of Color, these are natural spaces to consider when seeking to diversify the teaching force.

According to Petchauer and Mawhinney, MSIs are responsible for 38 percent of Black, 54 percent of Latinx, and 58 percent of Pacific Islander students who received undergraduate degrees in education.[18] And while it is true that MSIs have the potential to be powerful spaces that can interrupt current teacher demographics, enrolling large numbers of students of Color does not automatically lead to a healthy climate for students of Color. This is especially true for historically PWIs that have transitioned to being MSIs yet have made little effort toward interrogating whiteness within the institutional structures.

Julia, Gloria, and Leticia were three Latinas who were designated as English learners when they were young. When I interviewed them, they had just graduated with their teaching credentials and master's degrees from the same Southern California university that was designated both an HSI and an AANAPISI. Studying to become elementary educators, Leticia chose the university to stay close to family, but Gloria, a first-generation Chicana, and Julia, a daughter of Nicaraguan immigrants, had enrolled because of the program's social justice mission. Being trained to teach in local neighborhoods and placed on teams with supervisors of Color who seemed to care about equity and justice, they all expressed that they entered the program excited to become the teachers they felt their communities deserved.

Despite being in a program that is 67 percent teacher candidates of Color, however, these women experienced the climate in similarly hostile ways to how teacher candidates of Color describe their experiences in predominantly white teacher education programs.[19] Collectively, they shared how they were overlooked in class, their knowledge and insights were devalued, and they were consistently given worse grades than their white peers who also resisted critical discourse and centered their own experiences at the expense of learning how to serve communities of Color.

To highlight this culture, the women shared a specific moment from a class on family engagement taught by one of the only Latina professors in the program. Students were being exposed to what it means to serve working-class families of Color in a region that is more than 50 percent Latinx.[20] They had read Valencia and Black's article "'Mexican Americans Don't Value Education!'— On the Basis of the Myth, Mythmaking, and Debunking," and a white teacher candidate had been tasked with presenting on the content of the reading.[21] Instead of doing the assignment, however, she got up and challenged the focus of the class. Leticia began:

Leticia: She said she doesn't understand why all the focus has been on Latino or Asian families. That there are never any articles assigned about white families and their engagement, and she was very upset. She didn't go on to give us the information of the article—she just devalued the article. The professor was just shocked, trying to ask her about the article: like, who were the participants, and she was going around the questions, not giving her details.

This group of white students would always sit in the same area, they would comment, roll their eyes; they were so disrespectful in class. As a teacher, you want to respect your teachers. Right at seven, they would pack their bags and leave, even when we had a guest speaker. I felt like, "Are you serious? She is about to finish!" They would roll their eyes, they would talk, they would be on their computers.

Gloria: The reason I feel like they were not attentive is because they cannot relate. It's so frustrating because that class was so great in helping us expand our understanding, but those white students couldn't relate to the stories we were sharing. I shared a story on the first day about how my mom and dad as Latinos were supportive in different ways—they would cook for me at home, my mom would read me books, but they couldn't do more than that—they couldn't go to meetings, they couldn't do anything at school. And those students couldn't relate. I feel like we took that class because we want to learn about family engagement—we are Latinas, we wanted to learn how to engage with families in our community. But they took that class for credit, not for content.

Leticia: The professor talked about *consejos* (advice), building relationships, and how Latinx families show respect to their teachers. Yeah [laughs defiantly], they definitely couldn't relate.

Julia, Gloria, and Leticia were all committed to learning how to best serve families who, like their parents, may not have been recognized for their investment in their children's education. However, despite attending an HSI where Latinx students are the plurality and students are being trained to work in predominantly Latinx schools, the white students—who are the minority in this program—still asserted power when the course content did not meet their interests.

But as the racial minority in the space, where do white students get this power? As CRT informs us, whiteness is embedded in the laws, policies, and practices of an institution. And teacher education programs, even those enrolling mostly students of Color, are not exempt. The women shared how supervisors in the program—even supervisors of Color—were complicit with white supremacy. Among other actions, they (a) selected the only white students in the cohort to represent the program during mock job interviews with districts, (b) would call on white students more, (c) would give them more positive feedback, and (d) wrote them more positive letters of recommendation. The evaluation and belief system of what makes a quality teacher—even in this MSI where teacher candidates of Color were returning to serve in their own communities—was one that valued white students at the expense of teacher candidates of Color.

As schools were historically designed to control communities of Color through both curriculum and teachers who could foster nationalism and indoctrinate students into racial, cultural, and linguistic hierarchies, teacher education programs are also inextricably linked to this project.[22] Regardless of shifts in mission statements or changes in the demographics, until the structures of programs, the people hired to teach, and the content taught explicitly interrogate power and serve the self-determined needs of communities of Color, teacher preparation will continue to reproduce racism and marginalize critical teacher candidates of Color. Additionally, the preceding counterstories serve to highlight the *cumulative* racism teachers of Color experience in their K–12 education and then again in their teacher education, all of which serves to diminish their growth and the value they bring to the education system. Unfortunately, this racism does not end once they themselves become teachers.

K–12 TEACHING

Educational policies over the last few decades have determined a school's success by how students perform on racially biased standardized tests, even tying funding and resources to growth in measured outcomes for groups across race, language, and dis/ability.[23] The result has been an interest from schools and districts in the academic performance of historically marginalized students, who consistently score lower than their white and Asian American peers. Since research shows that the attendance, grade point averages, and college-going rates of students of Color increase when the content they are learning is relevant to their lives—and that teachers of Color increase their engagement and success—there is currently what CRT scholars have called an "interest convergence" for the recruitment of teachers of Color who teach in culturally responsive ways.[24]

Interest convergence, coined by Derrick Bell, argues that seeming progress toward racial equality occurs when the demands of communities of Color can be folded into the interests of whites.[25] He offers the example of Martin Luther King Jr. Day, an apparent victory for African Americans, as it honors the legacy of an important community activist. In reality, however, this symbolic recognition was a strategic concession by the government, as it appeased civil unrest without facilitating any material gains for Black communities.[26] Bell argues that this type of "progress" is actually surface-level change that does little to disrupt racial or economic inequities or hierarchies.

In the case of teachers of Color, Bell would likely argue that they are being recruited into public schools for their ability to engage students of Color in academic success because that is good for business (i.e., increased test scores). And while a focus on diversifying the teaching force can feel like a win for communities of Color, the interests converge conditionally. When teachers of Color begin to question or disrupt existing structures, it becomes clear that the institution is more vested in the existing (racist) structures than it is a diverse teaching force, and the interests diverge. In this section, I highlight the narratives of five critical teachers of Color who teach in four different cities. They are fighting for transformative educational opportunities for students of Color, but are racialized, silenced, and shut down by the very schools that recruited them: Rachel, a high school English teacher in Minnesota; Darnell and Jeffrey, two Black men who teach high school in the San Francisco Bay Area; Sonali, a South Asian math educator who taught in a charter school in Chicago and left to work in a public school in the Pacific Northwest; and Mateo, a Latino high school math teacher who works in eastern Washington State.

Rachel: A Challenge to Teacher of Color Relationality

An African American man from Baltimore moved to St. Paul, Minnesota, when he was in his early twenties and began working at a McDonald's. There, he met a young white woman and, as they like to joke, they "fell in love by the fryer." In the face of much resistance from their families, they married and had a biracial baby girl, Rachel.

When Rachel turned five, they enrolled her in a Catholic school and Rachel grew up as one of the only Black students throughout most of her education. As a highly social and relational person, she was often singled out by her mostly white teachers for being "too loud" or "talking too much." Even with a diagnosis and documentation of Attention Deficit Disorder once Rachel reached high school, the racist stereotypes teachers had about her character prevented them from accommodating her needs. Struggling academically, she grew up thinking that *she* was the problem.

With the support of two critical high school teachers who cultivated her analysis of the racism (and racist ableism) she was experiencing, Rachel became inspired to become a teacher.[27] She enrolled as an education major at a public university in Wisconsin, just an hour away. At this PWI in the Midwest, Rachel had classmates who proudly hung Confederate flags in their rooms and on the lawns. After just one "multicultural class," the teacher candidates were placed in public schools in Minneapolis to work with

Black and brown students. Her peers went reluctantly, expressing stereotypes such as "The kids were tough," and "They have
too much energy." She even heard, "It smelled in that building."
Reminded of racism she had experienced firsthand in her own
K–12 education, Rachel found college tough, but her students
were her refuge and she persisted.

Once Rachel graduated, she started teaching English at a high
school north of the city and became one of three teachers of Color
on a staff of 150. For the past four years, while she has had some
white allies on campus, she has found the climate very challenging, as many of the teachers do not well serve the 40 percent
student of Color population on campus. At a school with a significant number of Somali refugees, the teachers express xenopho-
bic sentiments, refuse to learn the names of students, and do not
even address the families. Rachel recalls an incident where a white
student poured a bottle of water on a Somali student's hijab; the
teacher who was present did nothing to intervene and there were
no consequences for this act of aggression.

In addition to the racism that Rachel witnessed, she herself
has also been subjected to many racial microaggressions. Teachers often talk to her about topics related to the Black community
to get her perspective as a Black woman, and they have called
her "aggressive" when she pushes back on their ideas or urges
the school to be more culturally sustaining. Rachel shared, "So
many people that I work with think that they are 'down' and
aren't racist, but when we really take a deep look at their practices,
curriculum, and their mind-set, they are not there, and they are
unwilling to be challenged."

Rachel has strong relationships with students of Color on
campus. She engages them in ways they connect to and, thus,

many students experience success in her classes. But her peers do not accept this. Rachel explained:

> I often feel like other teachers feel like I am not competent at my job because kids of Color like me, they do well in my class. I feel like they [the teachers] think I just pass them all . . . . After school, I usually have a cohort of kids of Color that just come kick it in my room, listen to music and hang out, and that's where they process all the racism they experience throughout the day. I'll sometimes have teachers walk by and you can just tell that they are not on board with that happening. I remember one time a teacher said to me, "Well, if the kids all like you, then you are doing something wrong."

Rachel approaches teaching through a sense of relationality—she cares about and feels an interconnectedness with her students—and, thus, provides them the space to connect and feel safe. She also teaches in ways that engage their lives and experiences. Most of the teachers at her school do not relate to students of Color and struggle to foster successful classroom experiences. Yet rather than acknowledging that Rachel is an effective educator, because of her positionality and approach to teaching her peers believe that she must just be passing students along.

Darnell and Jeffrey: The Burden of Insufficient Representation

Darnell and Jeffrey were both Black high school teachers in the San Francisco Bay Area of California, in the same urban district where Black students made up 28 percent of the population, but just 12 percent of advanced math enrollment, and almost

60 percent of suspensions and expulsions.[28] They both grew up locally, and after college, returned to be educators with goals of providing transformative educational opportunities for young people in the community.

Darnell was the son of a teacher, and when he moved home after attending a nearby university, he was excited to find a job where he could inspire students to engage in math learning. Once he started applying, however, the job search proved more intense than expected. Many of the school leaders and parents he met through his interview process had expectations of Darnell as a Black man that he felt went beyond his preparation and expertise. He shared:

> When I was trying to find a job, there was an overwhelming, "We really need you here to help our boys." I heard it from so many people that for me, it was like, "What if I'm not good at this? What if I'm not good at teaching math?" I don't want to be just a Black teacher, I want to be a good teacher. It was a big burden for me because I feel like "I'm twenty-five, I can't save all Black boys!" but I feel like I have that on me a lot and it's a lot of pressure.[29]

Because Black men make up just 2 percent of the teaching force and are severely underrepresented even in districts serving mostly Black students, a new Black male teacher like Darnell is tasked with additional responsibilities that his colleagues may not have. White women teachers make up the majority of new hires each year and are often exempt from the expectations of community engagement and mentorship.[30] Thus, they have room to focus on the steep learning curve of being a first-year teacher—developing their skills with curriculum, classroom systems, and pedagogy. While Darnell was also trying to master those key dimensions of being a classroom educator, he additionally had to shoulder roles—such as counselor, role model, and father figure—that he had not considered and had no training for. If the school and district had more veteran, Black male teachers, perhaps that overwhelming responsibility and pressure would not have fallen on Darnell.

Jeffrey was raised in the city, the son of a single mom. A fifth-year Spanish teacher when I interviewed him, he worked in a small charter high school downtown where the majority of teachers were white, and more than half of the students were Black. Reflective of the district data, Black students at his school were overrepresented in disciplinary measures and underrepresented in their graduation rates.

Jeffrey was committed to providing culturally sustaining curriculum that centered the needs of kids from his community, and he built into his curriculum the shared activist histories of Black and Latinx peoples. He was also invested in developing schoolwide policies and practices that would better address Black student engagement and success. A volunteer on the leadership committee, Jeffrey shared:

> Our leadership team is mostly white, with some Asian, Southeast Asian teachers. I have always been the only Black person on our leadership team the whole time I have been here. I'm the only one who speaks on African American issues and pushes the focus to serving African American students. I definitely feel that because of that, I have to represent even more and support every initiative because it would go unsaid and unnoticed if I don't say it.

While the engagement of all students at a school should be the responsibility of everyone that works at that school, no one except Jeffrey was advocating for the needs of Black students or the egregious inequities they were facing. Like Darnell, Jeffrey felt responsibilities that his peers did not have.

Exhausted by his invisible workload, he pushed for having more teachers of Color, and specifically more Black teachers. But administrators and teachers would respond with excuses to deflect hiring Black teacher such as, "They are not skilled enough," "There are not enough of them," or "But we can't hire them if there is somebody more skilled; we're not just going to go for them because they are Black." Two white male colleagues who shared these sentiments were always referenced as the "natural leaders of the school," yet Jeffrey was never encouraged to pursue formal leadership opportunities despite all of his extra labor and contributions at work.

Because of the severe underrepresentation of Black men in the profession, they were often positioned by non-Black peers and leaders with unreasonable responsibility to represent their race and attend to all problems related to race and racial inequity. Darnell endured racializing expectations that as a Black man he alone was to address the systemic disenfranchisement of Black boys, and Jeffrey was left as a sole advocate for Black students in the face of rampant antiblackness. In both cases, due to the burden of insufficient representation and the racial climate of their schools, these men were tasked with duties that spanned far beyond what the majority of teachers contend with—racialized labor that is relied upon yet is rarely recognized or rewarded.

Sonali: Charter Schools and the Diminishment of Teacher of Color Self-Efficacy

Sonali was born in Southern India, but relocated to the US when she was four so her father could pursue his master's degree in teaching. Her mother was without a work visa, and with little access to additional income beyond a teacher's salary, the family struggled to get by. Striving for their children's educational success in their Pacific Northwest community, Sonali's parents stopped cooking their native food or speaking their native tongue because they felt it would help them better assimilate with the dominant community.

They moved several times during Sonali's childhood out of financial distress, until her dad secured a job at an elite private school in Florida where she and her brother could attend high school for free. The transition from being in schools with working-class peers to attending a school with extremely wealthy, politically conservative, white students was a challenge. The school put European history, art, and languages on a pedestal, and her classmates would say condescending things to her such as, "You should be grateful that you even get to go here." These experiences throughout her childhood caused Sonali to internalize both a shame and a yearning for her cultural roots.

After high school, Sonali attended a large public university two hours from home where she majored in math and physics. As one of few women and often the only South Asian in classes filled with white men, she repeatedly witnessed racist and sexist comments and felt "othered." Interested in encouraging more young women of Color to enter science and math, she decided to become a teacher. During the fall of Sonali's senior year, some of her friends were applying to Teach For America (TFA). She had not heard much about the organization and did not know what charter schools were, but it was an economically feasible way to enter the profession, so she too applied and was accepted.

Sonali's six-week-long induction to the profession brought her to Chicago, Illinois, at a no-excuses charter school—a brand

51

of "achievement-oriented" schools that target working-class communities of Color with longer school days, a focus on testing, and harsh discipline. Sitting in site-based diversity trainings, Sonali began to realize that her professional development was steeped in deficit thinking where the overwhelmingly white teachers were framed as saviors to the Black and Latinx students. As she watched her peers evaluate students' progress and success against their assimilation to whiteness, her critical consciousness grew as she was reminded of her own negative childhood experiences.

After the summer training, Sonali was placed at another no-excuses charter high school. The floors were marked with tape for the teenagers to walk upon as they traveled from one class to another; students were shamed if their socks were not entirely black; and Sonali's assigned coach, having just completed two years of teaching with TFA before securing the job, had untenable qualifications. Sonali was being asked by administrators to script her lesson plans and engage in intensive test preparation, practices that felt unnatural and ineffective to the engaged pedagogy she was hoping to embody. She elaborated:

> My principal wanted scripted lesson plans, and I just couldn't do it—my brain just didn't work that way. And it wasn't because I wasn't working hard—I was working so hard. But it's just not the way that I think; not every student or teacher is the same, so you have to provide different ways for students to access content. She would also come into my classroom and videotape my entire lesson, and then she would pull me into my office and pause every three seconds and be like, "[This student] is done with his entry task, what's he doing? You have nothing for him! You are failing [him]."

The school's expectations and approach to supporting new teachers was one that made Sonali feel professionally inadequate. She continued:

> Because math is one of the subjects that schools heavily monitor, I felt so much pressure on me, and I felt like I was doing a bad job all the time. I was working ridiculous hours. My relationships with students were pretty good and I got really close to them, but it felt like I wasn't doing enough because my school was designed to make me feel like I was a terrible teacher. And I begged my principal to switch me to physics because it involves experiments, kids doing hands-on things. I begged her, and she told me, "We can't have what you did this year in a physics class."

The school promoted a sense of control and measured student and teacher success against numerous standardized assessments. There were many (mostly white) women who were seen as effective teachers because they followed this formula. But while Sonali did not have the language to articulate it at the time, she knew these practices were wrong.

With so much pressure and accountability, unmanageable hours, and no support for the project-based lessons she was trying to implement, Sonali felt pushed to the brink. She remembers that one Sunday she was trying to get in lesson plans for the week, and by 8:30 p.m. she still was not done scripting them: "I remember having a breakdown, and my colleague of Color was like '[Sonali], this is not normal, this is not okay. Scripted lesson plans? Don't be so hard on yourself.' And I didn't get them done, so I got pulled into my principal's office again." Sonali's worth and confidence as a teacher were repeatedly undermined at this school. Thankfully, during her second year, a woman who had been teaching in traditional public schools on the East Coast for several years joined the staff and started questioning the racist policies and practices of the school. She shared with Sonali that not all schools were this inhumane to students and educators. With this reframing, Sonali saw more possibilities in teaching and began to refuse the test preparation curricular focus more boldly.

After she had completed her time in TFA, Sonali applied to jobs back in the Pacific Northwest, wanting to go back to a community she felt more comfortable and connected to. With four years of distance, at a new school with progressive colleagues and more teachers of Color, Sonali reflected on how much she had grown in her embodiment of culturally sustaining pedagogy and project-based, collaborative math. Although she is still dealing with racializing challenges and barriers that come with working in schools, her hope and growth is intertwined with her students— working hard to hold onto her relational approach to teaching and invested in her community.

Mateo: Blocks to Systemic Change through Blocks to Teacher of Color Leadership

Mateo was born and raised in Mexico in a small village with little opportunity for economic stability. Following several of his siblings who went to the United States to seek work, he ended up, eighteen years old and undocumented, in a small city in eastern Washington State. Unlike many migrants, Mateo was fortunate to be able to rely on the food and shelter of his already established brothers and sisters for that first year. He arrived in January and, with limited agricultural work during those winter months, his brother enrolled him in English as a Second Language classes at the local community college. As he learned English, Mateo also began taking other classes and seemed to have a knack for mathematics. But with no access to financial aid at the time, he also juggled multiple under-the-table jobs for tuition and other expenses. Through the help of professors, counselors, peers, and the staff of student resource centers on campus, Mateo transferred and graduated from a four-year university with degrees in theoretical mathematics and Spanish. Before he graduated, he also got married and was able to become a legal permanent resident of the United States.

Carrying the values of his family and community, and as a member of *Movimiento Estudiantil Chicanx de Aztlán* (MEChA), Mateo was committed to a life of service and empowerment of his people and took a job as a high school mathematics teacher in a nearby city.[31] The district serves almost 70 percent Latinx students, many of whom are migrants, some who already work in the fields. For the past twelve years, Mateo has watched global conflicts and US policy and practices shape the demographic shifts of his students—from mostly Mexican in the past to predominantly Central American now—who often are seeking asylum from violence and a scarcity of the resources needed to live. Many of his students have experienced and continue to live with trauma as their family members are deported, they end up homeless, or they are forced to live or work in deplorable conditions. Coming from similar circumstances, Mateo relates to his students and their families, and he also understands their needs and their possibilities. He has been assembling an equity team that examines discipline practices, revises policies that systemically hinder the success of his students, and is developing plans to build a campus Dream Center to serve the needs of traditionally and historically underrepresented students.

Unfortunately, though, Mateo works among teachers who are 80 percent white and hold deep-rooted deficit ideologies of students and their families. He has heard teachers say, "We know how 'these' students are; we know they don't want to be in school. We know, parents, they don't want to listen, and they don't care about the education of their kids." These same teachers continuously resist his ideas for change and tell Mateo that he needs "to be a team player." Mateo, who has been an active in his advocacy throughout his tenure as a teacher, applied to several positions at his school to be part of leadership meetings, to voice his concerns, and to change inequitable policies and practices. "If I apply for a position, it doesn't matter if I am the most experienced, it does not matter if I am the most qualified, I will not get the job." Instead, white teachers and white principals, including those with little understanding or care for the Latinx community, are hired and promoted.

Now active in his union, Mateo shared how he is trying to organize for change, even without the support of his administrators:

> There is institutional racism embedded in the structure of how we run our school, and I am being perceived as a threat, as somebody who doesn't want to be a team player . . . . They [the teachers] feel like students just need discipline and academics, and for me, no. I believe we need to fulfill their needs first before we talk about what they need academically. They are not aware of the damage they are causing to the Latino population. I sometimes think about applying to a different position and just forgetting about it [this job], but I feel like if I leave, no one is going to advocate for the students. And more importantly, this system of oppression will remain intact.

As we see across the stories of Rachel, Darnel, Jeffrey, Sonali, and Mateo, teachers of Color are often sought because of their strong relationships with students of Color and their families. Ironically, policies and practices of traditional schooling often promote individualism and a detached approach to the profession that alienates these same teachers of Color from building upon their insights and strengths. They are often critiqued and pressured to dismiss the ontologies (ways of being) that they share with students and have developed as members of communities of Color.[32] This foundational conflict between how schools and critical teachers of Color operate has a detrimental impact on how they as teachers experience the profession.

THE PERSISTENCE OF RACISM

Racism is entrenched in the structures, culture, and climate of our educational system—K–12 and teacher education. From the time they were young to their pathway through the profession, critical teachers of Color faced messages that they do not belong in schools, that their communities do not deserve a quality education, and that they are not capable of being rigorous teachers or educational leaders. They confronted racial harm within school policies and practices, as well as endured microaggressions by peers and administrators. Some also internalized these deficit messages, believing that they were inadequate and ineffective.

Through the counterstories shared in this chapter, critical teachers of Color are speaking back to the racialized power structures of schools and teacher education. Like teachers of Color of the past that boldly stood to disrupt the racial and cultural hierarchies of segregated and government-sponsored schools, these educators endure a tremendous amount of alienation and disrespect to stand for what they believe families and communities deserve. Diverse across race and context, their stories display a deep sense of responsibility to create positive educational opportunities that reflect the histories, values, and cultures of students of Color. And while it is important to recognize the immense power and resilience of these educators, their stories must also remind us that simply diversifying the teaching force will not alter racism or the racial climates of schools.

3

"It takes a toll on you"

The Impact of a Hostile Racial Climate

M Y PARENTS EMIGRATED FROM INDIA to the US, and our family moved quite a bit when I was young. In my second-grade year, we ended up in the predominantly white city of Portland, Oregon. After school on one of my first few days, I went to the curb to be picked up by my mom. I was somewhat disheveled, carrying my backpack, sweatshirt, and a pile of artwork I was bringing home from class. My mom jumped out of the car to help, and as she hugged me, took my bag, and plopped me into the backseat, the cars behind were briefly blocked from driving away. An impatient father honked and started yelling at us to move. As my mom turned around and shouted to him that we were leaving, the white man roared in a voice so loud I felt all the teachers, kids, and their families could hear, "Go back to your own country!" We drove away and did not talk about it, but the fear I felt watching a man aggressively scream at my mother that we did not belong stuck in my mind.

Continuing on at the school, my brother and I endured actions and words—from teachers and students alike—that repeatedly framed our language, religion, and culture as inferior, deficient, and unwanted. We were asked if we ate snakes and were mocked and laughed at because a kid said we had been "shot in the head" when we wore *tikka* (a religious marking on the forehead) on a Hindu holiday. I was told in front of my teacher (who said nothing) that I shouldn't have a lead role in the class performance of *Mary Poppins* because my skin was too brown. Many of our encounters with racism at school were experienced as passing questions, "jokes," or comments uttered in an instance—often the very things adults around us would frame as casual ignorance before they would tell us, "Let it go."[1] But the accumulation of these racial assaults, despite how small or woven into the normal interactions of a day, had a lasting impact on how I saw myself as well as the world around me. By the time I left that school in sixth grade, I had rejected my home language and religion, was embarrassed by my family, and felt disdain for my skin—perceptions that stayed with me for many years.

Racism is more than an action, a belief, or the words out of someone's mouth. It is institutional power, driven by policies and practices that uphold inequities and injustices across racial lines; and it is also a social condition that impacts the material, psychological, and social-emotional well-being of people of Color. Frantz Fanon named the psychological impact of oppression as one of the most violent consequences of white supremacy, describing "people in whose soul an inferiority complex has been created by the death and burial of its local cultural originality."[2] The turmoil and struggle to maintain self, cultural, and community worth in the face of racialization is taxing, something that has been linked to high blood pressure and disease and likened to the combat fatigue experienced by soldiers in war.[3]

Although they often serve in schools with high populations of students of Color, teachers of Color work in a predominantly white profession that is governed by racist policies and practices. Carrying the cumulative impact of racism experienced in their own education and lives as they witness, endure, and confront racial harm in schools can be damaging in multifaceted ways that extend beyond the moment and context. In this chapter, I broaden the focus from the racialized experiences of critical teachers of Color that we explored in the previous chapter to examine and bring attention to the devastating impact of that racism on their personal and professional lives.

As schools recruit for teacher diversity, teachers of Color are often regarded for their abilities to effectively communicate with students and families, for good behavior management, or for delivering higher test scores. Although what undergirds these academic assets are teachers' political stance, relational approach to students, and transformational visions for education, (as we saw in chapter 2) these core attributes are often questioned and silenced. Thus, teachers of Color who stand ground for their communities actually endure more injury than is typically acknowledged. While the instances and impacts of racism are vast, I share the counterstories of six critical teachers of Color who were harmed and dispirited as their humanity and well-being were disregarded in their professional contexts. The teachers who are included expressly shared that they wanted their stories to be heard—but these narratives do include sensitive and possibly triggering content, including descriptions of racial stress, racial battle fatigue, and being pushed out of schools.

RACIAL STRESS AND RACIAL BATTLE FATIGUE

If you talk to most teachers in the US, you learn that stress is a typical part of the profession. Schools are underresourced and overcrowded, the workload is high, and teachers are underpaid. In the 2018–2019 school year, teacher strikes across the nation—in California, West Virginia, Oklahoma, Arizona, and Colorado—drew attention to a national crisis of these extreme conditions. A national poll on occupational stress found that almost half of teachers surveyed reported high daily stress, tying them with nurses for the most stressful occupation.[4] A 2018 study out of the University of Missouri found that 93 percent of elementary teachers experience extreme levels of stress that directly hinder their teaching and thus their students' academic success.[5]

Yet, within the arduous conditions of the teaching profession, teachers of Color are experiencing an additional layer of *racial stress*—stress associated with racism. From psychological research to a report from the US Surgeon General, it has been demonstrated that racism not only is stressful but also negatively impacts the mental health of people of Color.[6] Repeated exposure to racial discrimination or racism can compromise one's psychological and physiological well-being, as well as hinder one's ability to cope with stress.[7] Professor William Smith from the University of Utah has coined the psychological, physiological, emotional, and behavioral toll of racism on people of Color "racial battle fatigue," with symptoms ranging from social withdrawal, lowered aspirations, and exhaustion to anxiety, hypervigilance, anger, and depression.[8] Smith and his colleagues Tara Yosso and Daniel Solórzano explain: "The stress of unavoidable front-line racial battles in historically white spaces leads to people of Color feeling mentally, emotionally, and physically drained. The stress from racial microaggressions [and macroaggressions] can become lethal when the accumulation of physiological symptoms of racial battle fatigue are untreated, unnoticed, misdiagnosed, or personally dismissed."[9]

Thus, while teachers of Color are navigating the professional stresses that all teachers are experiencing—such as deprofessionalized wages, outdated technology, and large class sizes—they are simultaneously enduring racial stress that can compromise their health and well-being.[10] Here, I share the narratives of three justice-oriented Latinx teachers from California, a state where 55 percent of students are Latinx: Joaquin, a middle school history teacher from Sacramento; Carla, an elementary education credential student from the Coachella Valley; and Alberto, a high school world history teacher from Los Angeles. These educators bring attention to the racial stress and racial battle fatigue they endure trying to ensure a quality, culturally sustaining education for students of Color.

Joaquin: Isolation and Anxiety

Joaquin was raised in a small farming town in the Central Valley of California with parents who were active in the United Farm Workers movement. A light-skinned Latino, he was enrolled in honors classes with mostly white peers in a town and school that was overwhelmingly Latinx. His honors teachers had discouraged him from studying his own history, and even chastised him for hanging out with his closest friends and neighbors, whom they dismissed as "heading nowhere." Through the experience of being repeatedly othered from his community, Joaquin developed a dislike for school and a lack of confidence in his place there.

It wasn't until college, when he started to explore Chicanx studies and interact with kids who had been deemed "at risk" (as his childhood friends had been) through AmeriCorps, that Joaquin's interest in becoming an educator grew. Finding a connection to the stories of mislabeled and mistreated youth, he decided,

"I'm looking to be the teacher I needed when I was in school." He attended a justice-oriented credential program at a public university and eventually found a job at a middle school in the state capital of Sacramento.

Although the school served a diverse community of students of Color, it employed mostly white teachers. It was temporarily housed on a high school campus with no play space and was on its way to being closed. During its brief four-year history, five principals and numerous teachers had rotated through. When Joaquin walked through the door of his classroom on the first day, a student asked, "Oh, how long are *you* gonna last?" But Joaquin worked hard to engage his students innovatively and dialogically, and they grew to trust and respect him.

Joaquin's culturally sustaining approach was lost on his colleagues, however. He shared:

> They would make snarky remarks. Because of the way I dress and talk and interact with kids, shake their hands, teachers would say, "You need to tone it down. What are you, on their side? . . . Other teachers would tell me that they would talk about me in the staff lounge, that I can't control my class. To them it looks like chaos because they take the silent, traditional approach to teaching; and to me we are doing gallery walks, we are laughing, having conversations.

In the staff lounge, these same teachers who critiqued Joaquin's pedagogy called students "monkeys, bouncing off the wall" or "losers." They frequently blamed parents. Joaquin found himself pushing back, but he reached the point where it was so frustrating to be in the lounge that he stopped going there. The professional isolation, paired with an intense responsibility to advocate for his students, was taxing. He would wake up nauseous, not wanting to go to school, but feeling pressure that he couldn't take a day off because of how his students would be treated if he wasn't there. Joaquin spoke heavily:

> I was emotionally drained; it made me really tired. When I was in high school, my friends would tell me that the teachers would talk about me. And just knowing how that made me feel—I was one of those kids these teachers are talking mess about. And it takes a toll on you, frustrated, wondering, is this what being a teacher is? I don't want to be around this. I don't think I'm going to stay teaching. I don't think it's sustainable; the toll it's taken on my mental health is too much.

Carla: Extreme Stress

Carla was born in Mexico but resettled with her family in the desert of California's Coachella Valley when she was four years old. Throughout her education, she went to school with a significant population of Latinx students, but she never had a Latinx teacher. Daughter to proud Spanish speakers, she was vocal when she was young, but she attributes being a reserved adult to having teachers who viewed her and her community through a deficit lens. In seventh grade, her science teacher assigned her to sit in the back of the room. Although she had a strong grasp of the content and was ready to volunteer answers during class, he repeatedly ignored her when she raised her hand, and he ridiculed her and other Latinx students. One day, Carla finally shared her frustrations with her mother, who came in immediately to lodge a complaint with the office staff. The next day, Carla's teacher mocked her mother's limited English in front of the whole class. Shocked and disgusted by the extreme disrespect, Carla began to withdraw in school and lost any internal aspirations to continue. It was only for her parents, she says, that she pursued higher education.

Her junior year at a large public university, Carla took a few classes focused on issues of race, class, gender, and language inequities in education. With caring professors and new lenses to unpack power and in/justice, Carla began to problematize her educational journey. Newly impassioned, she decided to become a teacher. Similar to Joaquin, she articulated, "I wanted to be the teacher who would understand my students and the inequities going on in the school. I wanted to be that teacher I never had." Feeling reconnected to education through the relationality she had experienced from her undergraduate educators and the relational accountability she felt for students, she excitedly applied to the elementary teacher education program at her undergraduate institution.

At a Hispanic-serving institution (HSI) that develops teachers to serve the local region, the largest group enrolled in Carla's program were Latinx. Despite its demographics and social justice mission, however, Carla quickly realized that the program was not providing the tools she needed to be the teacher she envisioned. Her faculty advisor lacked adequate knowledge about the theoretical frames that drove her to the classroom and was unable to bring along her peers who were engaging in cultural appropriation and deficit thinking. She watched as the few white teacher candidates would receive praise for surface-level attempts to discuss equity, yet when she tried to assert her critical understandings, she was belittled and put in her place.

In her student teaching placement, Carla was paired with a teacher she did not feel aligned with. Carla shared how she had to sit through lectures where the class of students of Color were taught racist tropes, including "why Indian skin is red." She shared matter-of-factly, "I didn't want to learn what I was learning because I knew it wasn't good or helpful to the group of kids I was teaching." Upset that Carla was not adopting her approach to teaching, her guiding teacher eventually said, "If the principal asks if I should give you a job, I will say no. I think you should reconsider teaching; I don't think this is the job for you." Through tears, Carla reflected, "That totally broke my heart."

The marginalization that Carla was feeling was reminiscent of her middle school days, as she once again felt unsafe in her own education. With the long hours and intense workload, compounded with the racism she endured in her student teaching and graduate classes, Carla started experiencing chest pains. For three months she endured this recurring, inexplicable pain. One day as she was driving from student teaching to class, the left side of her body went numb. She thought she was having a heart attack. Scared, she checked herself into the hospital. After some tests, the doctors determined that the root was extreme stress and that she needed a break from all that was tension inducing.

When she emailed her faculty advisor that she was in the hospital and needed to take three days off of student teaching, her advisor replied, "Okay, we will need you to make up those hours next week." Carla was devastated, because "it seemed like no one cared."

Alberto: Broken Visions and Depression

Alberto is a second-year high school history teacher in Los Angeles, California. He grew up in a nearby working-class, gang-impacted community with underserved schools. With goals of affording a house in a better-resourced district, both his parents had multiple jobs—his father was a gardener in the morning, worked a grave-yard shift at a hotel every weeknight, and served as a janitor on the weekends. Because they worked so many hours, Alberto was not as close to his parents as to his older brother, who mostly cared for him. For middle school, Alberto was bused to a nearby community, where he was tracked into the honors program and had mostly Asian American and white classmates. There, he observed how few Latinx and African American students were enrolled, how negatively they were viewed and treated by teachers, and how little the curriculum connected to his own identity and lived experiences. Despite the negative climate, however, Alberto excelled, returned to his local high school, and enrolled in various Advanced Placement courses. He graduated valedictorian of his class and went on to attend a highly selective, world-renowned public university.

In college, Alberto entered as a science major but found his peers competitive and unsupportive, so his academic confidence began to plummet. It was not until he heeded the recommendation of his brother (who was now a teacher) that he enrolled in education courses and found a sense of purpose and community. For the first time, he was in dialogue with peers that shared aspects of his identity, discussing history and theories that explained the struggles and inequities they had all experienced growing up. It was then that he decided to become a history teacher.

Alberto ended up enrolling in a credential program at an elite private university that advertises a social justice mission and a commitment to underserved communities. He recalls, however, that he and the few other working-class teacher candidates of Color were jarred by the extreme whiteness and wealth of the campus, that most faculty and invited speakers were white and taught in wealthy districts, and, most significantly, that teacher candidates were funneled into those same districts for their student teaching and for jobs. Alberto graduated undersupported to navigate and thrive in urban schools serving students of Color.

After graduation, he decided to return to his community. Alberto secured a teaching position at a large high school that served 99 percent Latinx students, and where many of the teachers were also Latinx and from the community. Alberto started the academic year hopeful that this school was a fit because, as he said, "It felt like home."

In the first few months of the school year, he began to realize that, despite his sharing a racial/ethnic identity with these mostly older and veteran educators, there were significant ideological disconnects. He would hear teachers criticize kids for their postgraduate choices and disparage parents for not coming to campus for meetings or events, an absence Alberto could deeply understand. The principal did not investigate a letter signed by eight girls reporting the inappropriate behavior of a male teacher, but began enforcing random backpack checks of students. In addition, the most vocal teacher advocate for students, someone whom Alberto grew to trust and collaborate with, was not hired back for the next school year.

Within this egregiously hostile climate, as one of three world history teachers, Alberto was asked to align his assessments with the others. Unfortunately, they were teaching standards that were over fifteen years old, lauded a memorization of facts, and centered Europe in the curriculum—an approach in direct contradiction to Alberto's vision of teaching. When he veered from these standards and taught through more culturally sustaining, critical thinking, and dialogical approaches, he got in trouble with his principal.

For three weeks, my principal came into my room every other day and gave me evaluations—always saying negative things, reminding me that I was not aligned with the other teachers' [Eurocentric] standards. It was then I realized, Maybe I can't teach the way I dreamed? Maybe I can't teach beyond the white narrative at this school? Maybe I can't support students with critical thinking? It was really painful.

The conflict of wanting to keep his job teaching students in a community he cared for, but being surveilled, reprimanded, and forced to teach content that was not in their best interests, created significant stress for Alberto:

I would stress out at work a lot, and when I got home to do my work, I'd struggle to lesson plan. Forcing myself to align my teaching to the other teachers—or knowing that I'm not going to align it, but there's a chance she's [the principal] going to come in and see that I'm not doing everything they're doing and I'm going to get punished—that resulted in a lot of stress and anxiety. I stopped sleeping. I was eating my stress away, to the point that I became really unhealthy. I gained at least sixty pounds in one year.

The stress and anxiety provoked by the racial climate resulted in a lot of insecurity and depression for Alberto, something he had struggled with when he was younger. Alberto continued, with emotion in his voice:

Feeling alone in this place, I never felt like I had someone to support me. All together that made it really hard and . . . [a long pause as he got emotional and started to cry]

Me and my partner broke up. We were together for six and a half years, but the depression [I was feeling] was not something

70

I brought up, and she didn't understand all the things I was dealing with . . . [another pause and crying] . . .

It got really bad. I thought about committing suicide . . .

Last year really broke my vision of what teaching is.

Indigenous scholar Shawn Wilson explains that various Indigenous communities around the world approach life through a relational lens, where "an object or thing is not as important as one's relationships to it."[11] He also goes on to explain that these communities are defined by a deep commitment to those relationships. Wilson argues, "What is more important and meaningful is fulfilling a role and obligations . . . that is, being accountable to your relations."[12] Thus, one's life, he argues, is guided by what is good for the community.

Many justice-oriented teachers of Color also approach education through the lens of relationality and relational accountability.[13] Often teaching students from their own communities, from similar communities, or from communities of Color to which they feel political connection or allegiance, they feel a deep responsibility to the holistic growth and well-being of students. In the cases of Joaquin, Carla, and Alberto, they all expressed a strong relational accountability to the young people in their classrooms, wanting students to feel engaged and valued in their learning. Yet they carried this community orientation into schools fraught with deficit ideologies and disinvested teachers and administrators.

The counterstories also confirm that the presence of teachers of Color alone does not ensure a healthy racial climate. Joaquin, among predominantly white peers; Carla, with a white guiding teacher but in an MSI; and Alberto, among veteran Latinx teachers—all felt pressured to let go of their culturally sustaining visions for education and teach in ways they felt were harmful to students. Across varying degrees of racial representation, what was consistent was an epistemological conflict. How the critical teachers of Color in this book understood their roles, responsibilities, and drive as educators was in direct contradiction to the dominant culture of the schools. These experiences created significant racial stress for them, which resulted in racial battle fatigue that left Joaquin experiencing isolation and anxiety, Carla in the hospital, and Alberto contemplating taking his life.

TEACHER OF COLOR PUSHOUT

So what happens when the racial climate of schools is so harmful that it has psychological and physiological impacts on justice-oriented teachers of Color? How do they stay in schools that embrace policies and practices that directly contradict their visions for education and the world? The answer is that they do not always stay. Already in a profession with a low retention rate, as I shared in chapter 1, teachers of Color move schools and leave teaching at an altogether higher rate than their white peers.[14] And while teachers of Color have repeatedly shared feeling guilt for "abandoning young people" and shame for not being able to successfully resist or transform the oppressive conditions of schools, CRT reminds us of the role of institutional racism in maintaining a predominantly white teaching force. Critical teachers of Color are not just walking out the door of schools that they care so deeply about by choice. Schools that enforce disengaged curriculum and praise teachers who embody individualistic, dehumanizing pedagogies are designed also to reject the educators who challenge it; and the result is their systematic *pushout*.

Next, I share three counterstories of justice-oriented teachers of Color who—like Joaquin, Carla, and Alberto—pursued teaching to become the educators they never had, and to serve communities of Color in community- and culturally sustaining ways: Erin, a biracial Black woman who taught high school in Omaha, Nebraska; Emiko, a Japanese American transracial adoptee elementary school teacher in California's San Francisco Bay Area; and Andrea, a Puerto Rican elementary educator from Brooklyn, New York. These teachers also endured racism, racial stress, and racial battle fatigue, and in their cases, it resulted in their pushout from schools they felt deeply invested in.

Erin: Racial Bullying

Erin is a biracial Black woman in her twenties. Growing up in a mostly white town in South Dakota, she was the only Black student in her grade and one of a handful in the whole school throughout her entire education. Raised by her white mom and white stepfather, she had almost no exposure to Black family or community, yet the students and staff at the school continuously essentialized her as the expert on all things Black. In second grade, as the class was learning about slavery, a student suggested they could just ask their questions to Erin; as the rest of her peers laughed, the teacher quieted the class but said nothing to address the harm. In high school, when Barack Obama ran for president, students would make racist jokes and would refer to him as *Erin's* president. One day, her teacher had a lesson related to Black history and commented in front of the whole class, "Erin, you can help me out on this." In addition to being singled out as a Black knowledge expert, Erin also found herself often getting in trouble for not being able to sit still at her desk. Books and her journal became a safe escape from this hostile and "othering" climate.

When she got to college, Erin started tutoring young people and her time with K–12 students became another refuge. On the advice of some English education faculty, she decided to join her passions and become an English teacher. Wanting to be in a context with more people of Color, after she graduated she applied to teaching positions out of state.

A Latino principal from Nebraska began recruiting Erin to work at a large high school in Omaha, where of the eighteen hundred students, 83 percent were students of Color and 74 percent of students qualified for free or reduced-price lunch. She excitedly signed the contract, and when she arrived, the principal invited her and her mother to his house for dinner with his family. Erin recalled, "He was so welcoming and created a super positive environment. I was really excited about how this school year was going to start. It felt right."

When she got to the school, Erin realized that she was hired to be one of three teachers of Color out of ninety-nine teachers total. She was the only Black woman at the school, and one of the few across the whole district. She was also paired to co-teach several sections of her English language arts classes with a veteran special education teacher. This white woman was critical of Erin's culturally sustaining pedagogy, the strong relationships she had with students, and her restorative approaches to community building and discipline—all things Erin had learned in her credential program. This teacher criticized Erin to other teachers on campus, publicly undermined and berated Erin, and even discussed Erin's romantic relationship with students without her consent. "It felt like almost every single thing I did there was under a microscope. I started working in the library because I wanted to feel more comfortable, and then I was told by the principal that I couldn't work there. I lost over twenty pounds from just August to November. I was absolutely miserable. I cried every morning, I cried every night when I got back."

Under extreme stress, Erin sought help from her assigned coach, another veteran white woman educator. Erin confided in the teacher, sharing her professional struggles and the great anxiety they were causing her, to the point that she had gone to see a counselor. The teacher listened, offered some advice, and assured Erin she was there to help. When Erin returned to class the next week, her co-teacher told the students, "Ms. [Erin] is going to therapy because I'm too stressful for her."

Erin was shocked. She couldn't believe that her coach had broken trust in such an egregious way. This felt like the last straw, so she went to the principal to request that she be removed from working with her co-teacher. He replied that they just needed to "work it out." In her first professional job, away from all her family and friends, Erin tried to persist for several more weeks, but the stress was building and she felt so isolated. It was just too hard to be bullied by these older white women who were supposed to be supporting her, so she decided to quit. When she told the principal her plans, without any attempt to address the harm she had endured or improve her working conditions, he told her that she had signed a contract and that she would lose her state credential for a year if she broke it.

Floored by the lack of support and understanding of her need to leave, Erin turned to the union, but they didn't respond either. It wasn't until she sought the help of the African American dean of her college and another professor mentor that the district took her seriously. After weeks of battling, they finally let her out of her contract with her credential intact, and so Erin left the district and moved to another state once again.

Emiko: Administrative Apathy

The daughter of a Japanese mother and an Irish American father, Emiko was raised first on the East and then the West Coast. Before she finished elementary school, her parents passed away and she was taken in by their friends who lived in the San Francisco Bay Area of California. Suddenly living as a child of Color in an all-white family, Emiko was also enrolled in an affluent and predominantly white private school for the first time. Being in this new environment came with some "culture shock," as she described it. However, there were several teachers of Color at the school who were very supportive of Emiko. In particular, her English teacher—a Chinese American woman—began to mentor her and support the development of her voice in her writing. Emiko shared that the encouragement of this teacher and the few other teachers of Color at the school was foundational to her interest in being a teacher and to her personal identity, as their role in her life "had a huge impact on my identity formation as a person of color, a mixed-race person, and somebody who has something to say of value."

After high school, Emiko went to Japan for a year and spent time with her mother's side of the family. She returned to the Bay Area after college and enrolled in a small teacher education program that was guided by a social justice philosophy. Once a month, the program hosted a literacy event in the form of a community celebration. Emiko explained:

On the last Saturday of every month, we would advertise and lots of families in the neighborhood would come, and we would do these little literacy workshops and then have a big potluck and some singing or a puppet show—just something we would perform for [local] families . . . . We would cook the food and serve it, and it just felt like it was a beautiful community connection. It taught me the value of building those relationships with people in your community.[15]

This model of community engagement from Emiko's teacher preparation program became a foundational practice for her. After graduating, she secured a job across the Bay at an elementary school named after a Black activist that she admired. Serving a diverse student body, she learned that the students had been exposed to very little about the namesake of the school or about their own history. So, with several like-minded teachers at the school, she planned multiple events centered on the histories, cultures, and activism of Black and other people of Color.

Although the community was excited and engaged, the predominantly white teaching staff resisted and even undermined these efforts, expressing shame and embarrassment in celebrating such "radical" history. Emiko shared: "Every time I was trying to bring something to the community—the families were for it, the kids loved it, it was feeding their souls. And there was just the institution and the teachers who represent the institution and the dominant narrative, the oppressive narrative that kept trying to squash these community-centered, POC [people of Color]–centered kinds of events and celebrations." They began to personally target her, making it challenging for her to get things done at work, so she went to her principal and asked him for support.

Emiko said to him, "This is my school. I love this school. I want to stay here, but I can't stay here under these conditions. What are you going to do about it?"

But he did nothing. He responded, "It would be a shame if you left, but I understand if you leave."

Emiko ended up leaving the school. Reflecting upon her transition with emotion in her voice, she shared, "Making the decision to go was the hardest decision of my life. I firmly believed that I was going to stay at [that school] for the duration of my teaching career. I couldn't imagine being at another school. But I also could not live, year after year, in progressively damaging and oppressive conditions that were crushing my spirit."

Andrea: The Mental and Physical Toll of Racism

Growing up in foster care in Brooklyn, New York, Andrea describes herself as "a white-passing Puerto Rican in a Black household." As a young person, she had loved school because it provided her a constancy that she didn't always have at home. She was also really good at it, so even when she was missing days at a time, she could still show up and ace the test. In high school, teachers recognized her talent and encouraged her to apply for college. Writing was both a strength and passion of Andrea's, and her college essay landed her a full ride to a private liberal arts college, where she majored in sociology with a focus on prisons. It was in those classes that she developed a language for injustice and felt an agency for social change.

During her college journey, Andrea also became a mother. As she neared graduation, she felt nervous considering how she was going to support herself and her son. So at a job recruitment fair, she applied to work at a charter school network and, with her tutoring background, she was hired to teach at an elementary school back in Brooklyn—her home borough. She started orientation two weeks later.

This particular network of charter schools was notorious for its long hours, authoritarian leadership, and a revolving door of mostly white, unqualified teachers from elite universities who had little connection with the communities they served. Andrea entered her classroom filled with love, care, and a desire to engage the kids from her neighborhood in rigorous, relevant content. The students in her class were excelling academically, but as she got to know them better, she learned of their intense social-emotional needs. When Andrea reached out to the principal for help, she was told not to worry about it because the students were "achieving." In fact, the administrators were so amazed by the students' high academic gains that she was quickly promoted to be an instructional leader. Asked to teach others the 'secret to her success,' Andrea found it most important to confront the deficit and dehumanizing approach lauded by the school. Thus, she decided to lead a professional development series that explored power and identity, engaged with critical texts, and provided space for reflection on what it means to be a culturally sustaining educator.

But Andrea's answer to her administrators' and peers' call was not the silver bullet they had hoped for, and they resisted. When she spoke up for parents or kids or pointed out racial bias in the school's policies or practices, she was repeatedly disciplined— told she "lacked emotional rationality" and written up for being "unprofessional" with the threat of termination. In her first few years of teaching, Andrea was left emotionally drained by the task of bringing along the consciousness of a team of underequipped teachers in the face of this great pushback to her way of being. Andrea lamented:

I was always getting written up because of speaking up at meetings or telling leadership when things were not going as planned. It was this really weird tension that I felt where I was their model teacher. I was the exemplar. Every teacher they wanted to support, they sent to me. But at the same time, they invalidated my opinion and my thoughts. So, it's like they used me for the data they could get, but they didn't appreciate what I actually do.

One day, toward the end of the school year, Andrea was facilitating a professional development session from the culturally sustaining educator series. She had assigned the staff some prework and framed it as a no-technology space. The majority of teachers had not done the prework, and several remained on their phones despite her pleas for their presence.

In the back of the room, the principal and another teacher were giggling at pictures on a laptop during the session. Feeling a lack of respect for her labor and the cultural competence the students needed in their teachers, Andrea attempted to "call in" her peers at the next staff meeting, asking them to reflect on their disengagement.[16] She said to them, "I was left really discouraged. I'm not doing this work for myself—it's for our kids and it's a collective effort. I want you to take a moment to reflect on what it was about my session that you chose to refrain from, and I am open to talk more with anyone about this." One of the white teachers who had been on the phone began to cry.

The next day, Andrea was called in to speak to the administration. She recalled: "My principal put thirty seconds on her phone; she turned her laptop to me and had an email up that said, 'Andrea, as of today, you have been terminated.' She then said, 'You have thirty seconds to prove to me that this [my comments in the faculty meeting] was an emotional outburst and not a cal-culated decision, or I'm pressing Send.'" Andrea knew that the principal was feeling defensive because she herself was one of the people that had been disengaged. Wanting to defend herself but also feeling pressure to save her job, Andrea fumbled through her explanation. The principal responded abruptly: "Don't you dare ever try and undermine me or disrespect me in front of my team. You offended the white community, several teachers came to me crying . . . . It's not *what* you said, it's *how* you said it. We have spoken to you about this so many times. Next time I have to speak to you about your tone, it's *going* to be a termination."

Andrea reflected, "I remember leaving that meeting and breaking down. I literally had to say that what I did was unpro-fessional. It left me feeling extremely discouraged. It made me think, 'Maybe education isn't for me? Maybe I'm too radical to be a teacher? Maybe there are too many boxes of compliance that I have to check for the sake of checking them for someone else, as opposed to what our kids actually need.'" In the midst of this hostile climate, Andrea remained an invested advocate for her students—so much so that she felt this pressure to always be there to protect them from the harsh attitudes and discipline of other teachers at the school.

Andrea shared, "I had the fear of calling out sick. If I call out of work when I'm sick, who's going to watch my kids, what's going to happen, are they going to get suspended?" The intense pressure and responsibility she felt led this twenty-four-year-old woman to overlook her own health. She had been feeling an excruciating pain in her throat for a few days, but she kept pushing through because she felt like she needed to be there. After a week, she was feeling worse, as though she was going to pass out, but she still made it through the day. When she got home, she realized she had a temperature of 104.3 degrees and went straight to the emergency room, where they diagnosed her with septic shock—she had neglected an infection for so long that it spread to her blood and she was starting to experience organ failure. Andrea described it as "a physical manifestation of all the stress and anxiety," explaining, "I was literally almost killing myself for the job." With all the threats of termination, the stress of her responsibilities, and the realization that she had almost died and her son could have lost his mother, Andrea did not return to the school the following school year.

DIVERSITY AT WHAT EXPENSE?

"I started staying in my classroom at lunch."

"I dreaded going to work."

"I felt nauseous."

"I developed anxiety."

"I lost twenty pounds."

"I felt chest pains.

"I punched a wall."

"I felt alone."

"I wanted to take my own life."

"I didn't feel like I could call out of work."

"I felt like a failure."

"I stopped sleeping."

"I gained sixty pounds."

"I felt crazy."[17]

"I checked myself into the hospital."

These are all sentiments I have heard from the teachers of Color represented in this book and beyond. Students of Color deserve to have teachers that reflect them, and teachers of Color deserve a hand in shaping the education of their communities. Yet teachers of Color are often valued only for their material impact on schools—such as their ability to raise test scores and their effective management of students of Color—and are persistently over-looked, questioned, and critiqued for their humanistic value. As Andrea said, "They used me for the data they could get, but they didn't appreciate what I actually do." All too often, teachers of Color are not regarded as people with intrinsic worth; but rather, are treated as commodities useful only to leveraging the academic success of students of Color.[18]

Being alienated from their purpose, passion, and political goals can have psychological and physiological consequences for teachers of Color, as they often feel forced to choose between their ethics, health, and job, and thus they feel they must leave. Professor Marcos Pizarro and I, in a 2018 study about the racial battle fatigue of teachers of Color, explain:

> [T]hey felt immense responsibility to create educational environments where students of Color could thrive. This often meant confronting, challenging, and even striving to replace dominant paradigms alone, feeling pressure to be school "superheroes." They also simultaneously expressed feeling on high alert for the next racist encounter with a colleague or supervisor, and pressure to be hypervigilant in their work to protect both themselves from unwarranted critique and their students from psychic assaults. These constant stresses and demands lead teachers of Color to question themselves, to lose confidence, to lower their aspirations in the profession, and, as many teachers in our study mentioned, to end up leaving their schools.[19]

Similar to what we described in our study, the teachers of Color in this chapter carried an immense responsibility for their students and communities—to protect them from harm and to provide them the opportunity to thrive. Yet, as a result, the constant racism, racial stress, and racial battle fatigue they experienced was devastating to their minds, bodies, and spirits. As we consider diversifying the teaching force, we must also ask, at what expense? As students of Color make up half of the public school population and teachers of Color are needed to teach them effectively, educators and administrators must together hold the responsibility of interrupting racially harmful policies, practices, culture, and climate to make schools respectful, celebratory, and healthy places for people of Color.

4

"I don't want to back down"

Survival and Resistance

TEACHERS OF COLOR are urgently needed in the teaching profession. As we saw in chapters 2 and 3, however, in living their commitment to their communities, justice-oriented teachers of Color witness and endure a great deal of racism and trauma that takes a toll on their mental and physical health—to the point that many have to leave schools or teaching as a whole. Yet, while many committed educators feel unable to remain in the profession, there are others who stay. To unpack what it is that supports the retention of justice-oriented teachers of Color, this chapter is focused on those who survive the racial stress of the profession and are able to resist the injustices of schools. In their narratives, three tools emerge as foundational to their persistence: 1) *racial literacy*, understanding that the racial injustice they see, despite the denial of other colleagues, is real, structural, and ongoing, and that they have agency to disrupt it; 2) *communities of resistance*, finding others among whom they feel sustained in their struggles and transformative visions for schools; and 3) *organizing for change*, enacting their agency to reclaim and transform the education of communities of Color. In this chapter, I share the counterstories of seven teachers of Color whose reliance on these tools has contributed to their retention, growth, and transformative power.

RACIAL LITERACY

With an often-incessant barrage of racial harm and few colleagues who recognize it, justice-oriented teachers of Color can begin to feel that perhaps their analysis is mistaken or irrational. They begin to doubt their understandings, approach, or abilities, which can lead to isolation, marginalization, and attrition. On the other hand, having the capacity to identify the complex mechanisms of racism helps them to confidently assert their lens and demand shifts to policy and practice.

Harvard law professor Lani Guinier first conceptualized racial literacy as the "capacity to decipher the durable racial grammar that structures racialized hierarchies and frames the narrative of our republic."[1] In other words, it refers to a person's ability to recognize, name, and interrogate the racism embedded in our institutions. Guinier argues that to disrupt continued patterns of racial inequity, we must stop blaming individual prejudice for what is actually systemic racism. In the field of education, racial literacy has traditionally been applied to hold educators and administrators accountable to the needs of students of Color.[2] However, it can also serve as a mechanism of personal and professional survival for teachers of Color, as racial literacy enables a stronger analysis of how laws, policies, belief systems, and practices contribute to the racial inequities around them. Here, I share the narratives of three teachers of Color who strengthened their racial literacy from different sources in their lives—Karrie from her family, Imani in her undergraduate education, and Liza at a teacher professional development conference. They each gained knowledge that supported their capacity to say, "It's the system, not me," and this was instrumental to their sustained tenure as racial justice-oriented educators.

Karrie: Pedagogies of Family and Community

African American and Puerto Rican (or "Afro-Rican," as she likes to say), Karrie grew up as a second-generation resident of the Lower East Side (LES) of Manhattan. The LES in the 1980s was not the gentrified neighborhood of trendy bars and restaurants it now is, and she witnessed firsthand many people she loved passing away from heroin addiction and AIDS. Saddened by the struggles of her community, she would sometimes ask her parents if they could move somewhere else, but they would always tell her, "No! *These* are your people." She described her childhood as a cultural and political bubble, where everyone around her was politically progressive and reminded her regularly that her culture and community was beautiful and amazing. Karrie shared that when her parents asked about her future they never discussed money, but they would always ask, "What are you going to do to change the world?" She laughed as she remembered, "And honestly, I had that question drilled into my head since I was five years old."[3] It was in this context that Karrie developed her sense of self and purpose—that her community was powerful and that she had to live a life that gave back.

In addition to this solid foundation of self-love and relationality, Karrie's mother also taught her hard lessons about resistance at a young age. Her parents constantly reminded her that as a Black girl she had to fight to be respected in school. Karrie shared:

My mother, she never trusted teachers. I remember being told in first grade that I couldn't read, and they put me in class into a group called "the pigs." My parents were like, "Why are you called 'the pig'?" I told them right away that wasn't my choice, and I remember feeling like I really disappointed my parents. My mom turned to me when we got home and she was like, "First thing you have to understand is that every day, in that classroom, you are fighting, you are fighting to be there."[4]

Karrie's mother had an analysis of and a resistance to antiblack racism within the educational system, and she passed that form of racial literacy to her daughter.

As she grew up, Karrie lived her life through that perspective, and she proudly attributes her activism and success as a justice-oriented educator to those informal but intentional early lessons of her parents. Karrie eventually became a social studies teacher in a large comprehensive high school serving Black and Latinx students with many entrenched white teachers who carried deficit perspectives of students and cultivated a culture of low expectations. Always innovating in her own classroom through dynamic approaches to teaching critical history that included primary documents and inquiry-based methods, Karrie became known to justice-oriented teachers in the region as an educational leader. Yet she was often challenged by educators at her school who asserted limits on their shared students and fervently disagreed with her creative and relational pedagogy.

Karrie witnessed young people who were inspired and engaged in her class walk directly into demoralizing spaces with their next teacher, and she understood that the problem was systemic and that she had to do more. While the challenges of her school were draining and isolating, drawing from the strength and wisdom of her parents and community, she knew what it was like to be surrounded by love and cultural celebration; in turn, she had to fight for this vision in schools. With a team of critical educators across the district, Karrie secured an innovation grant and served as a key architect of one of the few explicitly social justice high schools in her city, helping to realize a racial justice vision that served the community. This space sustained Karrie's sense of purpose in schools, keeping her in the profession for over fifteen years.

Imani: Black Studies and Black Pride

Imani was a young teacher in South Los Angeles serving Black and Latinx students. Raised in a nearby beach city, she grew up in a space that was diverse, but with few Black peers. It was often said that "the schools are good" in that town, yet they were not "good" for *her*, as the curriculum was Eurocentric and neglected her Black identity. Being dark-skinned, she was also inundated with harmful messages of light-skinned beauty. But because her parents were deeply tied to their homelands of Uganda and Belize and she had spent time in both places growing up, although she could not name it at the time, she understood that these standards were flawed.

Seeking to know the history of her people, Imani became a history major in college, yet once again she was disappointed to learn that Black experiences were excluded from the curriculum. It was not until she added a Black studies degree that, for the first time, she had access to knowledge that centered the African diaspora. While she learned about the struggles and accomplishments of African Americans, it was the rich history of Africa that was most transformative to Imani. She explained its impact: "I began to embrace being from Africa more than ever, and I embraced my skin color more than before. I didn't feel like I needed to be light-skinned. I didn't need to have curly hair. If anything, I became more proud of not having those things because it shows that I'm more African, and I wanted people to know that."

Building on the foundation of her family, Imani's exposure to Black studies empowered her to reject the centrality of European knowledge, ways of being, and standards of beauty. She also developed an understanding of the role of Africa in world history, which profoundly shaped her approach to teaching.

The California Secondary Education Test (CSET) for social studies was a challenge for Imani, as it maintained a Eurocentric perspective. Her credential program also was not making sense of her pan-African frame in the training of social studies educators. Eventually securing a high school history teaching position, Imani was expected to rely on textbooks that continued to neglect the African continent. She also observed that students carried devastating misconceptions about the historical contributions of African people. Imani explained that she would begin each year asking them, "'What do you know about Africa?' and they would respond with, 'Oh, people are sick, people are dying,' all this negative stuff. Even the Black students would say negative stuff." And this broke her heart.

For many new teachers, the cumulative barriers to their vision serve as deterrents to persisting in the profession. However, because of the positive sense of self and racial literacy Imani had developed through exposure to pan-African studies, not only was she able to identify that the Eurocentric focus in the education system was problematic, but she also had the knowledge to disrupt it. She began to address the curricular disregard of Africa by changing the way US history was taught. For example, when she taught about slavery, she veered from the traditional approach of her colleagues that started with the slave trade. Instead, wanting her students to access the rich history of African people, she began her lessons with the ancient civilizations of West Africa, including Ghana, Songhai, and Mali, and shared that people came from all over the world to learn in Timbuktu. She poured effort into creating curriculum that would cultivate positive perceptions of Africans and their contributions to the world, and this approach challenged students and brought Imani much joy as a teacher.

Liza: Reframing Through Racial Theory

Liza, a queer Chicana, has been teaching for close to twenty years. A bilingual English educator at an alternative school in the San Francisco Bay Area, she has primarily worked with students transitioning out of the juvenile justice system.[5] Although a fierce social justice advocate and leader that is valued by students and their families, at one point Liza was almost pushed out of the profession. But instead, racial literacy was a tool that supported her survival and retention.

As a kid, Liza attended a predominantly white parochial elementary school and a racially mixed public high school, and she was guided by teachers and counselors who believed that Mexican American students were not intellectually capable of college. When she grew up and became a teacher, she was committed to being the teacher students of Color deserved. As one of few Latinx and Spanish-speaking teachers at her school, she developed close relationships with students and families and advocated for their needs.

Liza's peers, however, held deficit framings that reflected the teachers of her own K–12 schooling. They often engaged her through stereotypes about her own body, remarking that she was so tall even though "Mexicans are short and dark," or probing for why she did not have an accent. They would inquire why she was invited to confirmations or family baptisms, wondering if she was related to students. One teacher even asked if the reason Liza could connect so well to students was because she was in a gang herself.[6]

The racism she continually endured as a teacher was challenging, but it was also compounded by the racism she witnessed students experiencing and her attempts to disrupt it. When she spoke up against injustices she saw, other teachers would tune her out, and that led to feelings of isolation and depression. She was no longer sleeping well at night. She started stress eating. And it all culminated for Liza when, in her seventh year of teaching, her twenty-seventh student had passed away. Devastated by this loss—and the cumulative loss of young people she deeply cared for—she was at a breaking point and asked her administrators for bereavement time. She lamented:

> They were unapologetically callous. It was very matter-of-fact. "Well, [Liza], what do you think the work is? You know the students that you work with, and that's just what they do to each other." It was okay to them. "All of us here are working with the same kids. You're just taking it too personal. You need to distance yourself. You need to find a balance. Or, if you can't handle this—and this is the job—then maybe you should find another job." There was just no appreciation for the human life our students were.[7]

While struggling with the death of a student is a legitimate human response, her administrators told Liza that being disconnected was a necessary quality of an effective educator. Feeling alone

92

and unsupported, she eventually left the school and contemplated leaving the profession.

Trying to make sense of her experiences, Liza attended a professional development conference for educators focused on racism and racial justice in schools. There, she attended a talk on racial battle fatigue, a concept she had not previously known. As she heard the speaker liken racial stress to the stress soldiers feel in war—it can lead to depression, anxiety, loss of sleep, and more— she felt they were describing her. When the talk ended, she quietly raised her hand.

Called upon, she slowly stood up in a room of fifty strangers and spoke. She shared how her student had passed away, and that her administrators told her to care less. She then told everyone how the stress of that experience was so extreme that she couldn't get out of bed for many days, so she checked herself into the hospital to seek mental health support. She told the audience that she was thinking of walking away from teaching, but hearing the research on racial battle fatigue put words to her experiences, and helped her realize that it is the system that caused her to break down, not her own weakness.

That experience was a turning point for Liza. She began to read more critical theory and research, and she built relationships with other like-minded teachers to discuss the ideas with. She explained: "Reading about it, whether it's essays, books, or even blogs . . . talking about my experiences and actually having the tools and the words that I did not have before, has been very healing and cathartic in terms of like, you know, that I'm not paranoid and that I'm not crazy."[8] The strengthening of her racial literacy—the reframing of her experiences through racial theory—was a powerful force that helped Liza resist the narrative that she does not belong in the profession and grow even more strongly into the transformative activist educator she had dreamed of being.

Karrie, Imani, and Liza all encountered racialized challenges across their professional journeys—experiences that easily could have contributed to their disillusionment and pushout from the profession. However, one attribute that supported their persistence as educators was the racial literacy they developed from their families, communities, and critical learning spaces at various points in their lives. Being racially and ideologically isolated within a hostile racial climate can make teachers of Color feel irrational, that the way they understand the world is not valid or real, and this ultimately serves as a mechanism to maintain the status quo. Thus, surviving racism in schools and the profession must include a structural analysis of how systems, policies, and practices facilitate racial inequities and injustice.

COMMUNITIES OF RESISTANCE

> For one of the most vital ways we sustain ourselves is by building communities of resistance, places where we know we are not alone.
>
> —bell hooks[9]

Often it is the compounded experiences of racial isolation and ideological alienation that make teachers of Color feel as though they do not belong as educators, even in their own communities. In many spaces, the profession has been normed as unemotional, detached, and politically disengaged, and teachers who feel connected and accountable to the well-being of students and their families are challenged, shamed, and even pushed out of the profession. In addition to having a strong racial literacy, a key tool that has protected teachers of Color from the impact of hostile climates is, as bell hooks describes it, cultivating "communities of resistance"—collectives of activist-oriented people that remind each other they are not alone. Through the counterstories of Lamar, an African American elementary teacher from Virginia who attended a professional development conference explicitly for teachers of Color, and of Eva, a Dominican American high school English teacher from the Bronx who was part of a local teacher activist group, I show how building with other justice-oriented educators has emboldened teachers of Color to resist oppressive conditions and reclaim their power.

Lamar: An Affinity Space for Critical Teachers of Color

Lamar is an elementary educator in Fairfax County, Virginia, and has been working in schools for the last twelve years. Born into a military family, he moved around a lot until his parents eventually settled in a small town in Southeast Virginia when he was starting the eighth grade. Lamar had lived in a string of cities and schools within and outside the US—he had previously been one of very few African American students throughout his moves—and for the first time he was attending a predominantly Black school. While he was relieved and excited to be in a space with peers that reflected his racial identity, he soon realized that the city was fraught with a sordid history of antiblack racism. He now attended a school that was named after a Confederate soldier, he had predominantly white teachers who engaged Black students through stereotypes and deficits, and he experienced intense surveillance and control. In his first week on campus, he remembers being shoved up against the wall by a teacher because he was wearing a coat in the hallway—something Lamar had not known was against school policy. In that moment, it was actually a Latino security guard from the community that intervened and supported Lamar.

After graduating, Lamar attended a prestigious state university where he studied history. For the first time in his life, he learned Black history through an activist lens. He got involved with Black student groups on campus, organizing against institutional and everyday forms of racism. Although he and his Black peers were harassed by the police and were the targets of micro-aggressions and racist slurs, Lamar felt armed by history, in arms with his community, and empowered to resist.

His last semester of college, his father fell ill and eventually passed away, so Lamar moved home to be with his family. A neighbor, the principal of a local elementary school serving an entirely Black and working-class population, invited Lamar to support third graders with their reading. Lamar was paired with several caring and committed Black teachers whose approach changed the way he understood the profession. It was then that he decided to become an educator. Lamar soon enrolled in a teacher education program and landed his first job as a teacher in his community.

Throughout his career, he worked in schools in the region, and in every context he was the only or one of a few Black men. By his eleventh year, having served as an educator and an instructional coach, Lamar was very experienced and professionally knowledgeable. He was now a classroom teacher at a school serving many children of military families, but the demographics were shifting increasingly to students who lived below the poverty line and who read far below grade-level expectations. Leaning on his immense expertise, Lamar repeatedly brought up to the staff the urgency to shift their pedagogy and plan for the needs of struggling students, but his predominantly white peers went from ignoring him to resenting his voice. An instructional coach interpreted Lamar's comments as defiant and reported him to the principal for not following the curriculum that had been decided upon. Teachers started spreading rumors about his competence. His education, years of experience, and classroom success disregarded, Lamar felt isolated and started experiencing great stress and anxiety coming to work.

Seeking support, Lamar came upon the Institute for Teachers of Color Committed to Racial Justice—an organization dedicated to the racial literacy and racial justice leadership development of teachers of Color.[10] With no prior knowledge of the space, he applied to their annual convening for K–12 educators and flew to California that next summer. As he walked into the room of 150 teachers of Color from across the country, he heard music playing and people interacting, and he immediately felt at home. Connecting with other critical educators of Color, he realized, "It's not just me"—that he was not the only one challenged to navigate the hostile racial climates of schools. Lamar recalled one interaction that particularly moved him:

> There was one really young teacher that I met there, and I just remember feeling like, man, she's going through it. I'm thirty-five, she's probably twenty-two and she may not even stay in the profession. It made me put my experiences into context more . . . . I need to stay in the work and know more so I can make things better for the next generation of folks that come up. And that's kept me going; it's energized me.

Before attending, Lamar had not considered that anyone else was experiencing the school system as he had. As he continued through the space, he met more like-minded teachers who struggled as he

had, but had worked to challenge inequities across their classrooms, schools, and districts. Lamar explained:

> The last couple of years I had doubts about staying in the pro-
> fession. But with the tools, connections, and resources, some-
> thing about the experience pushed me to know more and think
> more critically about our education system and not just [stay
> focused on] my personal experiences. And now, I understand
> more where the things that I experienced came from, what they
> are rooted in, and I don't think that it's me.

Being part of a community of resistance helped Lamar to
see that the struggle of education existed beyond his experiences
or his context, and that realization was empowering. When he
returned to school that fall, things shifted. He shared, "For so
long I was afraid to speak up about these issues; I felt like I had to
teach correct history in secret. I felt a special eye on me from white
leaders. Now my hope, ultimately, is to have a bigger impact.
I don't want to back down." He started being more direct and
open, and having conversations about racism with peers and his
principal. He even spoke in front of the school board and district
superintendent.

> I started talking for the first time at faculty meetings about rac-
> ism in our schools, about injustice in our schools, and about
> the way that we do things. That led to a number of conversa-
> tions with my principal, and I have built some relationships
> with other teachers in my building because of that. I now say
> what needs to be said, and I never did that before. And I'm not
> holding anything in, so I don't feel stressed at work anymore.

Meeting other teachers of Color who are actively working to
disrupt injustice in schools at both classroom and systemwide

levels had a tremendous impact on Lamar's professional outlook, approach, and activism. It has aided in his retention, relieved his stress, and supported his capacity to resist racism in his school context and beyond.

Eva: A Teacher Activist Group

An Afro-Latina from the Dominican Republic, Eva grew up in the Bronx borough of New York City in a family that struggled financially. She went to a mix of public and Catholic schools and was primarily educated with working-class Black and Latinx peers, white teachers, and a curriculum that did not reflect her history or culture. She attended a local college, where she majored in English, but she always carried a love for science. After graduating, Eva took a job with an environmental justice organization, working with young people to build and restore urban farms. Taking this nonhierarchical and collaborative approach to engaging youth on critical issues, Eva found being an educator fulfilling, saying, "It felt like I was coming home." The joy she felt in the classroom led her to apply to an Urban Teacher Residency program where she would earn her credential while teaching full-time.

After a two-year stint at school Eva describes as "toxic," she wanted to return to her own community and secured a job as a high school English teacher in the Bronx. At a school that serves a diverse range of students of Color, she describes her job as "in many ways very powerful, and in other ways deeply damaging."

While Eva loves serving kids in her own community, she finds the climate racially hostile. Teachers have regularly mocked students' accents, and Eva witnessed a queer Black teacher who was loved by students pushed out because she advocated for their

needs and administrators found her too challenging. Unsupported by the union, Eva's colleague not only was asked to leave
the school but can no longer teach anywhere across the district.
Soon after, a student questioned why the principal brought in
only white teachers as possible hires and he responded, "It's hard
to find good teachers of Color." African American students have
also complained that paraprofessionals, guidance counselors, and
administrators favor Latinx students and have said things that
are explicitly antiblack. One day at a recruitment fair for new students, Eva observed the paraprofessionals—who are all Dominican women—being rude to an African American mother and her
kids. After the family left, the women came up to Eva and said,
"No queremos a esos negros en nuestra escuela." (*We don't want
those Black people in our school.*)

These experiences of racial harm would be hard for any caring teacher to witness, but they are that much more taxing for a
teacher like Eva, who is both Black and Latina, is from the community, and sees herself and her family reflected in her students.
So how does Eva survive and resist the hostile racial climate of her
school and profession? In her first year as an educator, she learned
about a teacher group that engages the critical literacies and collective action of educators across New York City schools. Attending monthly meetings and participating in Inquiry to Action
Groups (ItAGs) that met weekly for several months at a time, she
read about and engaged in dialogue with other educators about
concepts like racial capitalism and neoliberalism.[11] While many
teachers (like Liza and Lamar, for example) are not exposed to
critiques of structural racism in the education system until later
in their career, Eva was learning these frameworks as she was
learning to be an educator. She articulated: "I was learning how
to do a good *do now*, and also learning about racial injustice and

neoliberalism—all these things that I felt in my daily reality but did not have the language to talk about. It gave me the intellectual nourishment and really made me so passionate. Just to give people the space to do that is really powerful."[12] In addition to strengthening her racial literacy through exposure to texts and sustained dialogue, Eva also gained a great deal from being in community with other more experienced educators who shared her vision for critical and transformative education:

> It [the teacher activist group] connects me to elders in the community. They have been in this world for so much longer than me and being around that kind of wisdom, but also that enthusiasm and passion for justice, is just really inspiring for me. Our principal violates the contract in so many ways, and [a teacher in the group] is the [union] chapter leader at her school. She always tells me, "That's just not how that works." She gives me knowledge I would not have if I were not part of this space. I also cofacilitated my first ItAG last school year, and it gave me a lot more confidence that if I want to do something I can actually do it. I should have faith in my ideas—that if I have an idea and I am working with someone [like-minded] we can actually build something.

For Eva, being part of the teacher activist group was about learning the frameworks to name the inequities she was seeing, practice how to navigate and disrupt them, and also to imagine and build new approaches toward educational justice. Having this community of critical activist-oriented educators sustained and supported her professionally.

Communities of resistance for teachers of Color can take many forms, from formal membership in an organization to informal relationships with like-minded educators. Both Lamar and Eva found the communities they describe as part of critical professional development (CPD) spaces for teachers. Building from models of community-based education, CPDs are places of professional learning that frame "teachers as politically aware individuals who have a stake in teaching and transforming society."[13] They are designed to engage educators in dialogue, build solidarity, and provide shared leadership. From regular intimate meetings with a few participants (like the ItAGs Eva joined) to annual convenings serving numerous teachers (such as the racial affinity CPD Lamar attended), CPDs vary in who they serve and how they are structured, but they afford space for complex reflections and exposure to theory that heighten teachers' critical and racial literacies. Teachers of Color often rely on CPD when formal teacher education and school-based professional development fail to serve their political, cultural, and ideological needs, as it addresses isolation while strengthening their capacity to thrive and create change.[14] For Lamar and Eva, their participation in CPDs yielded communities for them that served to strengthen their analysis of injustice in their schools, supported their navigation of racism, and helped them strategize how to resist.

ORGANIZING FOR CHANGE

The third tool that emerged from the narratives of teachers of Color as foundational to their professional persistence is organizing for material change. It can be debilitating to think that the oppressive conditions many students of Color endure in schools must continue. In the same vein, there is hope and joy in believing that schools can be better, that communities of Color can realize culturally sustaining and engaging learning opportunities.

Building upon their racial literacies and their communities of resistance, many justice-oriented teachers of Color realize their visions in the profession through activism, demanding shifts in policies and practices to improve the educational conditions for disenfranchised communities. I share the stories of two teachers—Elena and Bayani—who engaged in organizing efforts across their districts to materially change the educational conditions of their communities. For both of them, their organizing also served as an important tool in their survival, resistance, and even purpose in the profession.

Elena: Unions and Strikes

Elena grew up in the Highland Park neighborhood of Northeast Los Angeles in a large Chicanx family. Her grandfather was employed at a bread factory that was unionized, and as a child she watched as he translated the union contract into Spanish and referenced it often to stand against management who tried to exploit the workers. Her father was a truck driver. He tried to unionize the company he drove for and was fired for his organizing efforts, but had always told her that he never regretted this. So, when Elena grew up and became a teacher in the second-largest district in the country, there was no doubt that she would join and be an active member of the United Teachers of Los Angeles (UTLA), as she had been raised to know the collective power of workers.

With a love for writing and for her people, Elena teaches English to all eleventh graders at a small public high school in South Los Angeles through a culturally reflective and social justice lens. The school serves 40 percent Central American, almost 60 percent Mexican, and a handful of Southeast Asian working-class students who live in a neighborhood with limited employment opportunities, health services, or social services. She and one of the US history teachers have co-created their own Humanitas reader to help students make meaningful sense of the inequities in their world. They include primary sources, research, and literature that confront dominant narratives, interrogate white supremacy, and explore the intersectional identities of many authors of Color.

Many of Elena's other peers did not understand or share her pedagogical commitments and were at times outright hostile. These teachers also did not express any urgency to address the ways the school itself was underresourced. Limited laptops and copy restrictions forced teachers to innovate with their assignments. They lacked both a nurse and a social worker on campus to assist students and families with their physical or mental health needs. "I wish I wouldn't have to tell my kids to not fall on Tuesdays because we don't have a nurse. We also need a psychiatric social worker full-time because our kids suffer a lot. I know that there are at least six families on campus that are experiencing homelessness, and there is nothing I can really do for them on school grounds. I'd have to refer them out." But Elena also pointed out that there are few community organizations nearby, and referring the families out would mean they would have to travel far outside the neighborhood. She just knew the district could be doing more.

As the union chapter chair at her school and a member of the political action arm, Elena also understood that her school was not alone in the resource issues it was facing. Although many local families expressed the view that charter schools were not serving the most marginalized of students, South and East Los Angeles were increasingly riddled with them. And thus, many public schools—like the one where Elena works—had been facing declining enrollment. Fewer students results in less funding, and as she said, "It started to really hurt our jobs."

Building on rent control movements in Los Angeles and a grassroots movement of teacher strikes nationwide, UTLA leadership planned a strike that culminated in January 2019.

> We hadn't received a raise in years, and you know how expensive LA is . . . . Our school board was mostly pro-charter. They would pass all the policies that would benefit charters and ultimately hurt our enrollment and our funding. That definitely unified us—the lack of resources. Fighting for more nurses, more psychiatric social workers full-time, and the end to random searches of our students—all of these social justice issues on top of our pay.

Elena shared that 98 percent of union members authorized the strike, and for six days teachers picketed in the rain for better policies and conditions for themselves, students, and families. While she worried about the cost of the strike to her own and other families, both financially and in terms of childcare, she felt lifted by a community. Each morning, her husband laid out thermals for her and her parents watched her daughter. Families came with food to support the teachers.

> I remember by the second day, I got to feeling really sorry for myself. There were no more rainboots in Los Angeles. I had ordered them online and I was waiting for them, so I put bags on my feet so they wouldn't get wet. And then you get on strike and you get real invigorated because everyone is there and they are in the same boat with you. I was on the loud horn, leading the chants. My role was to just get there, and no matter what,

let's have fun, let's eat together, let's chant together, let's walk together, and we will be fine.

Armed with racial literacy and a community of resistance, she organized to amplify the voices of teachers who were challenging harmful policies and practices across the district. And while they did not get all their demands met, they did have wins that felt "empowering" and "reinvigorating" to Elena.

I asked Elena about the impact striking had on her or her school context, and she explained that organizing for resources changed the teacher culture in her school and resolved much of the ideological isolation she felt:

> Before the strike, the culture was really bad and it was really isolating. And then we went on strike and all that changed. Now we are unified, I can talk to anybody, and they are receptive because I stood out in the rain for them for six days. We are on the same side—we now get that . . . . And now when I talk, even my colleagues that were resistant to some of these issues before, they are willing and understand. I'll have them sign a petition or walk with me and knock on doors, and they will totally do it because they now understand that that kind of engagement and organization is necessary.

Bayani: Teacher and Community Solidarity

Bayani is a Pilipino high school English and social studies teacher in Stockton, California.[15] The grandson of a farmworker and the son of a single mother, he grew up in the diverse central California city in the historical neighborhood Little Manila—where Pilipinx agricultural workers from the 1930s onward developed a bustling community as a response to racially discriminatory laws that prevented them from accessing the white business district. The neighborhood is now shared with working-class Southeast Asians, Sikh Punjabis, African Americans, Pacific Islanders, and poor white families.

Bayani's K–12 schooling reflected the diversity of the community with his peers and to some degree with his teachers, but never in the curriculum. While there was a public perception of the city as a violent, crime-filled region, throughout his education there was no mention of the rich local history of community activism and resistance, and no remnants of ethnic studies that had been established in Stockton schools in the 1960s. It was not until late high school (through a mentor) and in college at San Francisco State University (through ethnic studies classes) that Bayani was introduced to the organizing power of the Pilipinx community in Stockton. And through a sparked curiosity, he started to learn of his own grandfather's involvement with the United Farm Workers Movement. The critical lenses of ethnic studies helped Bayani make sense of the impact of structural racism on his community. He was shocked and angry that all of this knowledge had been kept from him, but he also began to develop a purpose in challenging it. As his racial literacy strengthened, he asked, "What would have been the difference for myself if I knew more about myself? If I knew how much my grandfather sacrificed for us, for our country? . . . Youth need to know they exist and their existence matters, that they are part of society."

With his newfound lens, Bayani applied and was selected to an organization within his university, Pinay/oy Educational Partnership (PEP), an ethnic studies teaching pipeline in San Francisco from kindergarten through college.[16] Through regular planning meetings, summer trainings, and retreats, Bayani and the other PEP instructors collectively innovated dynamic curricular approaches to teach ethnic studies in predominantly Pilipinx schools. They also socialized, ate meals together, and became a family in the movement to transform education. And for the first time, through PEP, he experienced the joy and power of teaching and organizing.

Through this experience, Bayani decided he was destined to be an educator and wanted to bring liberatory practices to his own community. Thus, after attending a social justice–oriented teacher preparation program in Los Angeles, he felt beyond thrilled to accept a high school teaching job and return to Stockton. But his excitement quickly waned with the realization that he was now immersed in a context with mostly white teachers, with a scripted curriculum, where he felt he had no like-minded colleagues to build and plan with. The racism and the stereotypes teachers expressed to students and Bayani were rampant, and colleagues seemed woefully unaware of the transformative possibilities of education. So the responsibility he felt to young people had him arriving at school earlier than everyone, staying later than everyone, planning every day during the first half of his winter break—and the racial stress of being a "superhero" for his community started to accumulate. One day in the spring, the racial battle fatigue became too much and Bayani ended up punching a wall—he had used so much force that he had to have his hand wrapped for many months. In retrospect, he reflected, "There are definitely other ways that I could have dealt with the problem but in the situation, because I had no community I could rely on at that moment, I felt so isolated."[17] After three years of that stress, Bayani eventually left the school.

But he did not leave the profession. Bayani—now an eighth-year teacher—was hired at his high school alma mater. In this newer professional context, students also experience deficit perceptions and overt racism from teachers and counselors. But now, Bayani has educator allies across the city. Applying the organizing skills he had developed through PEP, he began building a small cohort of like-minded teachers at different schools—having meals, going for hikes, and discussing their vision for education.

> We have been very intentional in building camaraderie, checking in, planning together, and organizing together. Now when we have questions and concerns, we have that allyship. We will text each other, "Can you believe this happened?" A couple months ago, an army recruiter tackled one of our students on campus. It was hard to find people to talk to about that [at my school] . . . . But something like that happening, just being on my own, it would have been really hard . . . . Our cohort, luckily, was a space we could talk about that, and basically talk about the military industrial complex. We also spoke out against it.

From his college days, Bayani had learned to build meaningful relationships and organize toward a transformative vision of education for his community. When he had first arrived in Stockton, he was missing that community of resistance, and he experienced a great deal of racism that took its toll on him. It was not until he rebuilt community toward this transformative purpose that he began to feel supported, strong, and empowered to resist.

Bayani and his teacher allies have now been organizing with various community-based groups across the city—from Black student unions to the Native American Center, the Chicano Research Center, a Sikh *gurdwara* (temple), and the organization ICE Out of Stockton—to pass a resolution where ethnic studies will be a requirement in all high schools across the district.[18] They have held community meetings and also involved a school board member to ensure that the process was transparent and a community effort. This collective organizing work has helped Bayani realize his vision for education and his community, and also has served as a catalyst for his survival and resistance, as well as his happiness and enjoyment of the profession.

Elena and Bayani both developed tools before they became K–12 teachers to organize for change—they had strengthened their racial literacies and learned of the power of community, which carried them through hard times at their jobs. Elena through the union and Bayani through a more grassroots approach both built upon their critical analyses of structural inequities and leveraged the collective the power of teachers. And in both cases, the process shifted the culture of their schools, as well as district policies and practices.

MOVING PAST SURVIVAL TO RESISTANCE

The counterstories of seven teachers of Color included in this chapter bring to light mechanisms that teachers of Color can rely upon to survive and resist the impact of racism in schools and the teaching profession. These teachers, diverse in positionality, geography, and approach, all struggled within hostile racial climates; and where their colleagues were pushed out, they instead were able to push for transformation. Three key tools emerged from their stories.

The first tool was racial literacy—critiques of structural racism that were cultivated both organically through family and community or through formal exposure in their education or organizing work. Racial literacy enabled the teachers of Color to put language to the inequities they observed and to be confident and systematic in their confrontation of racism. This aided in their professional survival because they were able to resist messages that they were sensitive or irrational. The second tool builds upon their racial literacy, and is being part of a community of resistance—meaning being connected to other educators who share their critiques of injustice. This tool helped them realize that they are not alone in their struggle, which combated feelings of isolation that often precipitate teacher pushout. The third tool is organizing for change, where teachers of Color leverage their racial literacy and communities of resistance to build movements toward educational transformation. Organizing with other educators toward policies and practices that are more culturally sustaining and racially just helped teachers embody their sense of purpose in the profession. Through these three tools, teachers of Color were able to refuse the dehumanization and cultural disregard of schools, and collectively fight to reclaim education.

5

"To dream with others"

Reimagining and Reclaiming Education

WHEN I WAS A MIDDLE SCHOOL TEACHER years ago, I took a summer class on urban education at a local university to fill in some of the theoretical and research holes that my credential program had not addressed. My professor presented us with a reading describing a classroom with desks and chairs, a teacher in the front, and students sitting in rows. He asked us to guess when the text was written. While many thought the 1950s or 1960s, it turned out the piece was authored in the late nineteenth century. The students in the class, myself included, were shocked that the structure of classrooms has remained so unchanged for over a century.

Womanist scholar AnaLouise Keating describes status quo stories as "worldviews that normalize and naturalize the existing social system, values, and standards so entirely that they prevent us from imagining the possibility of change."[1] US public schools are among those status quo stories. Although chalkboards and chalk have shifted to smartboards and laptops, the social systems, values, and standards that govern our educational system have remained so constant that we have normalized the impossibility of meaningful change. Thus, when people talk of the dilemmas of schooling, they frequently discuss improving students' performance within the existing system. Consequently, money is poured into programs and initiatives that are targeted to improve students' educational outcomes, with little attention to how the structure itself is actually flawed.

There is a lineage of critical scholars, however, who have spent their careers calling out systemic oppression in our educational system, pointing to how our laws, policies, and practices uphold racial, classed, and gendered hierarchies. Throughout this book, we have also seen teachers who powerfully rely on their political analysis, their community orientation, and their collective organizing to resist the oppressive structures of schools. But fighting against unjust institutions—particularly when the injustices are so normalized—is unrelenting, exhausting work, and those who engage can become drained and disillusioned by the battle. For Black, Indigenous, and people of Color to be whole in a system so fraught with antiblackness, settler colonialism, and racism, it is essential to consider a life beyond opposition and resistance.

THE NEED TO DREAM

I inherited my mother's belief that the map to a new world is in the imagination, in what we see in our third eyes rather than in the desolation that surrounds us. Now that I look back with hindsight, my writing and the kind of politics to which I've been drawn have more to do with imagining a different future than being pissed off about the present. Not that I haven't been angry, frustrated, and critical of the misery created by race, gender, and class oppression—past and present. That goes without saying. My point is that the *dream of a new world . . .* was the catalyst for my own political engagement.

—Robin D. G. Kelly[2]

Robin D. G. Kelly, in his book about the Black radical imagination, reflects on his mother's unwavering dreams of, as he shares, "land, a spacious house, fresh air, organic food, and endless meadows without boundaries, free of evil and violence, free of toxins and environmental hazards, free of poverty, racism, and sexism . . . just free." He grew up listening to visions of possibility, of a different and better way. And wrapped up in this utopic imagining was a map of sustenance, peace, and liberation.

As educators struggle for the well-being of students of Color and their communities, it is important to take up Kelly's call and dream beyond what we are fighting *against* to what we are fighting *for*. What does a classroom look like that is humanizing and racially just? What is a pedagogy where students of Color feel seen, nurtured, in relationship, and whole? What does learning look like when it is meaningful and connected to students' lives? This type of dreaming—of what communities of Color want, need, and deserve for their youth—is foundational to realizing something different and better.

This chapter presents the counterstories of five veteran critical teachers of Color who have boldly reimagined schools for and with communities of Color, and have brought their visions to fruition. The first three teachers have engaged in this radical imagination in their classrooms: from curricular and pedagogical changes to epistemological shifts. The second two educators have reimagined on a district level, building teacher of Color coalitions and establishing ethnic studies for all disciplines. As a collective, these teachers show us the possibilities and promise of an education that centers the humanity, epistemologies (ways of knowing), and ontologies (ways of being) of students of Color *and* teachers of Color.

REIMAGINING CLASSROOMS

One of the key places that teachers can dream is in their classrooms and with their students. I share the narratives of three teachers of Color from differing positionalities, disciplines, and experiences who have reimagined the structures and boundaries of schooling: Salina, a middle school science teacher who has built upon Black radical traditions, humanizing pedagogy, and restorative justice approaches to support the growth of Black and brown scientists; Lelei, a Samoan elementary educator from Hawaiʻi who has centered within her pedagogy Indigenous knowledge systems that include land and ancestors; and Christina, a high school English teacher who has facilitated yearlong research projects to nurture her students in East Los Angeles as community activists and leaders. Each woman built her classroom not only into a place where her students could grow, thrive, and be whole, but also into a reimagined space that was pivotal in her own retention, growth, and healing.

Salina: Restorative Science Pedagogy

Salina is a Black middle school science educator in Southern California who has been teaching for the last twenty-four years. When she was just nine years old, she decided she was going to be a teacher after watching an interview with a famous Black educator,

Marva Collins. During her youth, Salina's life was fraught with instability as she moved often between her mother and grandmother, traveling to and from Northern and Southern California. And while she didn't stay in one school for very long, do much homework, or get good grades, she was a strong reader and writer and school was always a place she really enjoyed. In high school, Salina had several key educators that believed in her and exposed her to Black writers, filmmakers, and thinkers that fostered her critical consciousness. So, when she finished twelfth grade and moved to Texas to attend a historically Black college, she was already committed to a life of Black empowerment.

Salina had a gifted mind, though she came to college without some of the strategic study skills and tools needed to navigate her education. Indeed, it was caring Black professors who supported and encouraged Salina to make it through. She graduated with a major in biology and a minor in chemistry, and promptly enrolled in a teacher education program where she taught for a year in Texas before returning to Southern California.

For Salina, coming from an environment that valued Black brilliance into a Los Angeles area school that had a limited vision of education for Black and Latinx students was a significant challenge. While she did not have the language for it at the time, she was relational, engaged in trauma-informed pedagogy, and built upon the context and lives of her students to teach environmental racism. While the youth felt deeply connected to Salina, select parents and the majority of other teachers at the school persistently questioned why she was talking about race, gender, and social issues in a *science* classroom. They felt she was not following the curriculum, and they questioned her methods and expertise. They submitted written complaints to the local school board and tried to get her fired. As Salina's students thrived and excelled, she felt under constant attack because, as she put it, "the world wasn't oriented to support who I was trying to be" as a teacher.

But then a local professor invited Salina into a community of justice-oriented educators from across Los Angeles who met regularly, studied critical theory, and discussed how to teach toward liberation. For the next few years, Salina's confidence and capacity grew as she was in relationship with other teacher "disrupters" and developed language to articulate what was inherent to her practice. One day, sitting in a movie theater watching a powerful scene of a Black scientist saving the world in his laboratory, Salina thought, "I want every Black kid in the world to see this scene." As she reflected further, she gained clarity on her vision—she wanted to support the growth of young Black scientists grounded in repairing injustices in the world. That day, Salina decided to pursue a PhD in science education.

Entering a doctoral program in an elite, private university as an experienced educator and a critically conscious Black woman was not an easy road. Salina remembered: "I came in talking about race and identity in science. I had a couple of professors ask me to stop using the term *white supremacy* in my papers, saying things like, 'This language is problematic.' I had several people try to check me in public spaces." Black women teachers make up just 6 percent of the teaching force, and a much smaller percentage of science teachers. A *critical* Black woman science teacher—one who builds connections between structural oppression, race, and science—was beyond what her program seemed ready for. But eventually, Salina found an intellectual and pedagogical home with her advisor, a few close peers, and the teacher education program. In collaboration, she built out a framework called (W)holistic Science Pedagogy (WSP) that engages the Next Generation

Science Standards, is humanizing, and is guided by principles of restorative justice that encourage accountability to repairing harm and restoring community.[3]

While most of her colleagues pursued university positions after graduation, Salina instead excitedly returned to her Black and Latinx community to apply the guiding principles of WSP to the middle school classroom: "A commitment (1) to an ever-developing self-awareness, (2) to science and its practices, (3) to science as a transformative agent, (4) to their students' social emotional wellness, and (5) to restorative practices."[4]

Salina begins from the premise that the students of Color in her classes are already scientists. She articulated: "The root of *science* means 'to know,' and so I tell my kids that you all already are scientists. If you ask questions and you're trying to find answers, if you are testing things, that is the essence of what science is. So more than me connecting science to the world, it's facilitating an experience where they connect who they are to the content." Salina also understands that their lives as young adults are beset with social-emotional struggles, social injustice, and education content without connection, so she strives for a classroom space where they are seen. Salina declared, "I want my students to feel loved. That's essential, crucial, the first order of every day." So she starts each class, every day—even in the rain—standing outside her door to greet each of her 120 students. When Salina takes attendance, she tries to connect with everyone individually. She is strict but strives to be authentic and transparent with her approach and expectations, creating an environment for rigorous learning where students feel whole. As they shuffle between their six classes in the day, students often have nowhere to process all they are carrying; but with Salina, they trust her and they feel safe. She holds restorative circles where anyone can share what they are struggling with. In her class, students have revealed their sexual identity to their peers, they have shared that they are being harassed, they have asked for help with cutting and depression—because they know their experiences and feelings will be taken seriously as Salina makes time to process it all. And while this appears to some as unnecessary, "noninstructional" time, Salina argues this approach actually allows for deeper learning: "This means that when we do science, which we do every day, we get a lot more done because the kids are able to focus and want to do it. I'm not having to stop the lesson and discipline. When we do science, we're on to science, and the kids end up learning."

Salina holds restorative practices as a foundation to her classroom culture and supports students to apply those same frames to science content. For example, when teaching a unit on water, Salina has included lessons on water contamination in Flint, Michigan. Students are tasked with understanding the water cycle and the biological and environmental necessities of water, but also to understand how government decisions have created public health crises that have destroyed the lives of Black and working-class people. Salina guides the lesson through restorative justice questions, asking: What was the harm? Who was harmed? How do we repair the harm? Can the harm actually ever be repaired? Through this approach, the students not only learn the molecular and biological knowledge of water, but also understand the relationships among water, life, power, and in/justice.

In the US educational system, Black and brown students are often marginalized from dynamic science content; they are underrepresented in science majors and advanced degrees and, thus, are kept out of careers in science and medicine. Black and brown communities are also overrepresented by the impacts of environmental racism and health inequalities. Through years of deep study and a vision for her people, Salina brings a racially literate, restorative approach to science that inspires Black and Latinx students to grow as the scientists she knows they already are, and the scientists the world needs.

Lelei: Centering Land and Legacies

Lelei is a sixth-grade educator and has been teaching elementary school for eighteen years. She identifies as an Indigenous woman of Samoan descent who is connected with nature, the elements of the world, and its creations. She was born and raised by first-generation Samoan immigrants in the working-class Kalihi neighborhood of Honolulu on the island of Oʻahu in Hawaiʻi. As the eldest child, she helped to raise her sisters and numerous family members who migrated to the US system for economic opportunities. Although she was steeped in her language and culture when she was young, school became a force undoing her Polynesian ways of knowing and being in the world. She, her siblings, and her cousins were enrolled in an English as a Second Language program, and through being drilled and repeatedly corrected by teachers in English grammar and vocabulary, over time, her whole family began speaking English as their primary language. Lelei laments that, as they pushed their youth toward academics and good grades, her family left many Samoan traditions behind. In high school, she joined a Polynesian club, and the cultural connections she garnered from that space led her to add a Polynesian studies minor to her science major in college. Still, Lelei felt that pieces of her identity remained compartmentalized.

When she graduated from college, Lelei had dreams of traveling the world and applied to teach English in the Philippines. But she was the first member of the family with a college degree and they needed her to financially provide now that she had graduated, so she declined that position and applied for opportunities within the Hawai'i Department of Education. Thus began Lelei's teaching career. At the time, Lelei felt buried under her familial responsibilities, so when she was finally able, she left for California. But after five years of teaching on the mainland, she yearned for the island, her family, and the way of life in O'ahu.

Lelei returned to Hawai'i older, more experienced, and with a deeper sense of identity and purpose to serve her community. Simultaneously, she was more aware of the contradictions and harm of the schooling system and struggled to find a sense of belonging in teaching. She shared: "The Department of Education is very Westernized in ways where we can't really exercise our [cultural] practices because of the demands that are put on us, the type of curriculum that we have to teach, the assessment scores that we have to meet. A lot of the demands were too heavy for me, and there was no way for me to be myself and the teacher I wanted to be." Lelei joined a district team tasked to make the curriculum more culturally responsive, but these efforts were limited to superficial edits, such as replacing "squirrel" with "fish" in math word problems.

Frustrated that she was ill-serving the youth of her community, Lelei had contemplated leaving the profession until a coworker introduced her to the University of Hawai'i summer Ethnomathematics Studies program—a place-based approach to math content that builds upon local and Indigenous historical traditions, culture, and knowledge systems. Nine years into her teaching career, Lelei finally felt "awakened," "empowered," and whole as she learned to align her professional work to her community and movements on the Island. Through ethnomathematics and a network of likeminded teachers, she felt capable of centering

the evaporating knowledge of her ancestors and reclaiming education as a healing space for young people. Lelei explained:

> A lot of things have been happening within our community,
> with rights being taken away and injustices to the land. I'm liv-
> ing in a time where we have protectors now, advocates, who are
> reminding us we are not going to stand for it . . . . It is time
> for us to take a stance in having our children grow up and
> know who they are and who they came from. That's the sense
> of belonging. We always talk about the trauma of this genera-
> tion, but there is so much healing when we are able to learn
> the culture of our people. And if it's not now, then there won't
> be a tomorrow.

Lelei began to shift her teaching practices to embody the epistemologies and ontologies of her people. She worked tirelessly with
the support of her ethnomathematics community to reimagine
what school felt like for students.

Now, every morning when they arrive, the kids leave their
shoes outside like many do in their own homes. Lelei and the students start the day by asking permission to be on that land; they
chant or sing songs of their place, they declare their values, and
they contemplate a daily Hawaiian proverb. Whenever possible,
Lelei and the students visit natural settings to understand what
they are studying, and they spend time each day learning outside.
For example, when they were studying coordinates in math, they
took aerial-view pictures of the class garden to locate different
plants or locations using graphing and geometry. For science, they
visited streams and tested water quality, as well as worked with
local farmers to learn about static hydroponics in growing taro.
When they studied ruling systems in social studies, Lelei paired
these topics with an "I Am a Legacy" project, where students

explored the genealogy of a family member as a means to understand their intergenerational connectivity and collective greatness. And Lelei visits each of her students' homes once a month to make sure her connection to her students is also with their families.

The learning of Lelei's class is grounded in shared cultural knowledge, collectivity, and relationality. And because of the deep bonds they developed, her students—many of whom had been suspended from school and were constantly referred out of class the year before—are now highly engaged. Numerous students entered the year limited in their reading and math but soared in her class because she taught those subjects through doing and being with the land. At the end of the year, they showcased to the school what it means to learn from the land and have the land teach you, and Lelei beamed as she described how it felt to watch them share their understandings from a place of confidence and belonging: "I can totally see that they're different. From sitting in the chair for long hours to them being outside doing a task or figuring something out, I see how much love they have for their education and passion they have when they are discovering or investigating things. I see an explosion of light and pure happiness in school when they are able to learn that way."

While her administrators had initially tried to bring Lelei back to the traditional approach and test preparatory curriculum, they also now see the powerful, far-reaching impact of her work. Lelei has leveraged the wisdom of her ancestors, protectors, and community to transform her classroom into a place of joy and connectivity for students who had previously felt disenfranchised. Her engagement with land and legacies is humanizing and invigorating for her students, and this work to reclaim education has had a deep impact on her as well. Lelei proclaimed, "You can't teach someone else to love something or someone if you're not loving yourself. At a time, I didn't know myself. That's what I'm learning too." Together, she and her students are beginning to reclaim their power and their place in schools.

Christina: Youth Research, Leadership, and Activism

Christina is a fifteenth-year high school English teacher in East Los Angeles. As a second-generation Korean immigrant, she grew up in the 1990s in a suburban neighborhood in Orange County, California. She attended a well-resourced magnet high school that was primarily white and Korean, where there were two computer labs (before these were a norm in many schools) and students left campus each lunch period to buy food from local restaurants. Viewed through the model minority myth, Korean students at the school were expected to be studious and succeed academically while they were simultaneously invisible in curriculum, sports, and school leadership. But Christina did not fit into this school culture—she did not excel in her classes or feel connected to her teachers—and eventually she dropped out.

Christina's parents were incredibly disappointed in her decision and the tension in her house was high, so she moved in with her older brother in Oakland, California. There, she enrolled to finish her degree at a local public high school that served primarily Black students with a small population of Southeast Asian refugee youth. The school was at the top of a hill and locked its tall gates every morning once the students arrived. Armed security officers surveilled the halls, and a police car parked in front of the school all day. In class, moreover, Christina was being tasked with content she had learned four years earlier at her previous school.

With such disparate opportunities at these two schools, Christina developed a growing awareness and anger of systemic inequity and injustice. After graduating high school, she started taking classes at community college and found Asian American studies. For the first time in many years, Christina's passion for learning was fueled as she learned of structural oppression and resistance in the histories of diverse Asian American and other racialized communities. Her grade point average climbed as she re-engaged in school, and after a few years, she transferred to UCLA to major in Asian American studies, invigorated by a drive for social change. Through an Asian community leadership class, she was placed to work in a Koreatown youth center and decided that teaching was a way to live her deeply rooted goals. She decided, "I'm going to be the teacher that I didn't have."

After attending a justice-oriented teacher education program, Christina took a job at a historic East Los Angeles high school within an economically disenfranchised Latinx neighborhood, known as a hub of activism. In a context far different from those she had grown up in, Christina still felt a connection to the students. She explained, "I know what it's like to have a mom who doesn't speak English and to have to translate for your parents. I know what it's like to be perceived as a foreigner, or not see yourself reflected in the dominant culture." Grounded in her own identity, however, she also understood that despite her years at the school, she was still a visitor in the community. Christina clarified, "I don't feel like I'm Latina. I don't need to be with a bunch of other Asian American people to feel Asian. I'm here to do work. I'm here to push justice forward."

Thus, with political purpose and the spirit of cross-racial solidarity, she has provided rigorous educational opportunities for students to develop as community leaders. She says to her students, "Dream big! You could be at the United Nations; you can be making all kinds of policies. There's no reason why you can't get into these institutions and destroy them. And don't wait for me because I'm not the leader. I'm an outsider; I don't want to lead your community."

Christina began collaborating with other politicized teachers at the school—a group of them started meeting at the end of the day to read educational research and theory, lesson plan, and discuss critical issues on campus. In 2009, when the great recession economically decimated California and K–12 educators received a Reduction in Force (RIF) notification in record numbers, teachers and students across the district began organizing against the layoffs. The students in Christina's class had many questions about why this was happening. It was after testing; there were three weeks left in the school year; and while many teachers were just having students watch movies, Christina and her colleague Maria wanted the kids to do more. A few of their peers had been engaging with Youth Participatory Action Research (YPAR)—"research conducted 'with' as opposed to 'on' youth, around the issues they find most important in their lives."[5] So Christina and Maria jointly decided, "We'll just have the kids research what is happening; because we could give them our biased opinion, but having them ask those questions is so much more important."

The Los Angeles Unified School District had just started partnering with nonprofits to manage their local districts, and charter schools were on the rise. The kids were put onto teams and tasked with learning about the various stakeholders and conditions that led to this moment. They began answering questions such as: What is a district? Who are these partnership organizations? What are their agendas? Christina and Maria then held mini-workshops for the class to teach each other. The students left this project feeling empowered with a deeper understanding of the changes happening around them, and some of them even began organizing to resist a charter school colocation on their campus.

With so much student excitement and learning, Christina and Maria decided to build this pedagogical approach into their curriculum each year. Three years into the project, the principal—who was very supportive of their work—agreed to let them stretch the research into a yearlong interdisciplinary project for juniors held in their English course. He also connected them to a geographic information system (GIS) company, where they were trained to build mapping into their curriculum.

Over the years, the project has evolved to a schoolwide expectation, where juniors spend the year learning to use community mapping as a way to identify and analyze the structural roots of inequitable conditions in their neighborhoods. It culminates with them presenting their findings to their peers through student-led conferences. Students have engaged in projects that not only have resulted in high-level learning that has garnered them awards and invitations to share their work locally and across the state, but also have contributed to important changes in the policies and practices that shape their communities. One group, for example, created maps of the air quality, freeways, and greenspace of various schools across the district, demonstrating the poor conditions that disproportionately impact working-class Black and Latinx communities. In fact, United Teachers of Los Angeles leaders used these maps during their 2019 union strike (referenced in chapter 4) to negotiate an investment in grass and trees in the playgrounds of South and East Los Angeles schools. Another group worked alongside an environmental protections nonprofit and won the fight for toxin testing in the soil around a factory in their neighborhood.

A third group of students included Citlali, who identifies as queer and brown. The group's first task was to decide on a critical issue to research, but they were struggling for days to choose one. Christina always pushes her students to reflect on their own experiences when considering what to study. Finally, Citlali asked, "Why does my sister always go into 'Check into Cash' places?" She wondered why there were so many predatory lending places in their community. From there, the group began to ask questions about economic disenfranchisement, the historical roots of racial and class segregation, and eventually redlining. Christina describes how the group ran into class one day bubbling with excitement, "Miss, do you know what reverse redlining is? We read three books, and there's this guy from Harvard [who writes about it]." They explained that reverse redlining is when a bank charges people of Color more than white consumers in a non-redlined area. The group then began to ask questions like: What does it mean that people of Color were forced to live close to freeways? What does it mean for their health? What does it mean for financial justice? They were able to create interactive maps that showed historical redlining and how it correlates today to a lack of parks, limited economic opportunities, and lower academic attainment.

Citlali shared that she felt genuinely cared for by her teachers, and she was so moved by the power of geographic patterns that this project forever changed her relationship to education. She expressed:

> I came into the class and I didn't know what research was, but there were constant check-ins, scaffolding, and reflections of social issues in the community. Whatever knowledge I already have despite my lack of familiarity with research and academia, Miss [Christina] constantly validated what I did know.

The research pertained to myself, to the people I knew in my community, to my family, my ancestors. There were things I already knew and things I already felt, and just bringing that into the space, it was just very validating. And that's when I began to think, you know, despite how many times these voices have been thrown away from academia, I am smart. I have something to contribute.

By facilitating a rigorous, yearlong engagement with research, Christina's approach to teaching supported students' growth academically and as agents of change. They emerged from her class with concrete inquiry skills and as leaders investigating, reflecting upon, and addressing issues of structural oppression within their communities. They left with a stronger sense of self-efficacy in their intelligence and capability.

This journey of teaching YPAR with students has also been reciprocally impactful for Christina. She shared: "Working with students has been a healing and humanizing process for me. Looking back, I was so angry as a young person and even as a younger teacher I entered the classroom looking to disrupt and dismantle the system. But a lot of the things that drove me were my feelings of anger . . . . But [the students] taught me to really love and feel hope, not to just be mad at the world."

From Salina's vision of humanizing and restorative science education to Lelei's centering of her and her students' shared knowledge systems and Christina's fostering of students' self-efficacy to disrupt injustice in their own community, each of these powerful teachers of Color has resisted the deficit, Eurocentric, and culturally disconnected ways of learning that are rampant in schools. Dreaming beyond the fight, they have reimagined and reclaimed their classrooms as holistic, dynamic, creative spaces where students, and they themselves, can heal and grow in multidimensional ways.

REIMAGINING SCHOOLS AND DISTRICTS

Salina, Lelei, and Christina's transformative pedagogies demonstrate the power of reimagined classrooms. And still, there is a broader sociopolitical climate of laws, policies, and practices that also shape what is possible across a school or district. Next I share the narratives of two teachers of Color who dreamed and worked to realize schools and districts filled with teachers of Color who reflect and honor the assets of communities of Color: Ramona, a midwestern elementary educator who reimagined her school and district through coalitions of critical teachers of Color, and Julian, a high school English teacher from a California desert town who has collaborated with educators and community members to realize a district with ethnic studies courses across various grades and disciplines. Together their narratives show the power and possibilities of justice-oriented teachers of Color on a systemic level.

Ramona: Teacher-of-Color Coalitions

In her mid-sixties with curly gray hair and an amiable smile, Ramona is a mother, a grandmother, and an elementary school teacher of over twenty years. From a paternal lineage of farmworkers, she was raised in a tightknit Mexican American community in Texas where she recalls a *Tejano* cultural pride at home and a family feel at school as teachers embraced the community and cultivated strong relationships. Ramona's father was not always around, so her family eventually moved to a mostly white midwestern community to be near her maternal grandparents. Ramona brought along her bilingual tongue, and when she spoke on her first day of fifth grade, a student loudly jeered, "You talk funny!" Her new home came with major adjustments in language, culture, and community, and although Ramona eventually adapted to this different space, she missed the warm feeling of her Texas roots.

Her whole life, Ramona had taken care of her four siblings, and the consistent family message was that she should go to college and become a teacher. One day in high school, several activists who had been organizing with César Chávez were tabling outside of a grocery store. Talking with them, Ramona remembered her father's stories and was inspired by their work; for the first time, she found clarity for her future. She decided, "I wanted to teach kids from backgrounds like me." After two years of community college, Ramona received a scholarship and finished her education degree. She eventually got a teaching job in a small working-class town serving migrant Latinx students alongside many teachers of Color from the community.

Although she felt she was doing what she set out to do, after a decade in this work, Ramona left the classroom to teach overseas and pursue other things. When she returned to the US years later with a wealth of experiences and her critical lens, she began teaching in a small district on the outskirts of St. Paul, Minnesota. In a state with one of the largest academic disparities in the nation between white and students of Color, teachers of Color make up just 4 percent of the teaching force.[6] In Ramona's district, most educators and school leaders were heavily focused on traditional measures of achievement, with meager attempts to address racial and class inequities. While Ramona was serving students of Color in her classes well, she knew they were experiencing harm in other classrooms and she felt compelled to respond. But as she brought forward culturally sustaining and equity-focused initiatives at her school, her principal worked to quell these attempts for systemic change and eventually pushed her out. One year later at a new school, the justice-oriented principal she had gone to work for was pushed out. The racial battle fatigue she felt from these barriers to equity and justice work was so debilitating, she took a leave of absence.

During her time at home, Ramona considered moving on from the district and the profession, but then decided she had to come back. She explained, "I just felt called back to this place and to these people. Like a phoenix, I'm just going to keep coming back. This principal—you gave it your best shot to get rid of me, and you didn't. And I know you are afraid of me now! I've reached a place in my life where I don't mind speaking truth to power, and helping other people learn how to do that as well—on behalf of themselves and on behalf of our students." Ramona returned to the district and took a position at a Title I elementary school where she teaches now, serving a diverse range of students of Color, including many Vietnamese, Hmong, Karen, Nepali, and Somalian refugees. The predominantly white educators of the district began teaching long before the demographic shifts of the neighborhood, and are limited in their competencies to work with the current student population. Within this professional context, Ramona has continued to lead efforts to advocate for communities of Color and has also invested in recruiting teachers of Color to the school. She has supported these new Black, Latinx, and Asian American educators in their racial literacy and collective power, bringing them together to ask, "How are we going to address this inequity? What are we going to do?" And so recently, when a group of white teachers at the school proposed "World Cultures Day" during Spirit Week, where students were to "dress up like a country or culture they would like to visit"—a practice that can essentialize cultures and lead to appropriation—Ramona and her colleagues organized a unified response to argue to the staff why this was racist and harmful.

While the collective strength of the growing group of teachers of Color has been instrumental in resisting racism at her school, Ramona has never forgotten the empowering feel of her elementary education in Texas. And so, she dreams beyond an antiracist education, where her energy is put toward disrupting harmful events or experiences, toward creating schools that value the languages, cultures, and epistemologies of students and their families. With the support of her administrators and a districtwide equity advisor, she began to write grants. In three years, she brought in over $125,000, which she has used for course buyouts so she can have time away from the classroom to lobby with legislators for teacher diversity, build networks with other critical educators across the state and country, and bring critical initiatives back to her community.

One practice that Ramona dreamed and realized was an intercultural family circle. Parents who did not speak English had historically met in affinity spaces grouped by language with a district liaison who served as a translator for school-based initiatives. Isolated by this approach, parents of diverse race, language, or culture rarely had time together or with teachers. Ramona felt that to realize her community-responsive vision of education, collective dialogue was needed. The district liaisons were resistant at first, arguing, "It isn't going to work." But Ramona insisted: "Let's just try this!" She brought Nepali, Karen, Latinx, and African American parents together with teachers using translating headsets that she funded through her grant. In a circle, they sat, told stories, and listened to one another. It was powerful for varying communities to see their commonalities and their divergent struggles and strengths, and for teachers to experience translations and learn from parents with whom they typically did not directly communicate. The success of the event led the district to fund and adopt the model.

Along with teacher leaders from three neighboring school districts, Ramona also reimagined professional support for teachers of Color through a mentoring program that centers their identities and needs. She shared, "Teachers of Color come with great heart, passion, and skills to change a system that didn't work for them. Part of our work is helping teachers move back authentically into who they are—their roots, their ancestry. That's the groundedness they need to keep doing this work." Operating like mutual aid, the districts pool their resources and build a wider network that 1) supports the growth, racial literacy development, and success of teachers of Color, and 2) trains veteran teachers of Color as mentors to support the induction of new teachers of Color. For example, if a new high school math teacher of Color needs support navigating the racial climate or advocating for critical curriculum but there are no veteran educators of Color with that knowledge or expertise in their district, they can access veteran educators of Color from any of the partner districts for support. In addition to teacher support, this cross-district collective has also written a report identifying race-based inequities and recommendations on how to support students who are Black, Indigenous, and people of Color, which several districts have partnered with the group to adopt.

A powerful force, Ramona has endured a great deal of hostility in her struggle for a humanizing education that values students and their families. It is through her persistence, collaborative approach, and reimagination that educators at her school are now organizing to resist racism, that families are being heard, and that teachers of Color are working across district lines to collectively reclaim their power and agency to transform schools. Ramona identifies that the work has also been a gift, being able "to dream with others, and through our tenacity and skills, [see] those dreams become reality."

Julian: Ethnic Studies Across the Disciplines

Julian is a high school English teacher in the Coachella Valley of Southern California that was born from a lineage of Chicana/o/x activists. His grandfather was part of the Los Angeles Zoot Suit Riots of the 1940s, many of his *tías* (aunts) and *tíos* (uncles) were involved in the United Farmworkers Movement and the Chicana/o Power Movement of the 1960s and 1970s, and one of his *tíos* helped to establish Chicano Park in San Diego. So, as Julian recalls, conversations around the dinner table were recurrently about critical consciousness, social awareness, and self-determination in the face of a racist system: "Inside my house was a lot of love, a lot of care, a lot of support, a lot of history, a lot of centering of who I am."

But when he would walk out the door of his home, the narrative about him, his community, and the world was completely different. Alicia, Julian's mother, was a vocal advocate and one of few Latinx educators in their hometown within a sea of white teachers and administrators. Throughout elementary school she served as his protector from injustice and harm, but once he went to sixth grade, that drastically changed. Julian described the demeaning comments from teachers as relentless, with the constant message of, "You're not going to succeed. You're brown and Mexican, and you're going to end up dead, in jail, or shot." Often sent to the principal's office without reason, teachers would say, "See? I told you this was going to happen," and at times they would block him from returning to class, preventing him from accessing his education.

In seventh grade, Julian was enrolled in a drafting class where they drew two-, three-, and four-dimensional figures and he was really enjoying the curriculum. One of the assignments was to build a plane. They had to draft it with real measurements, and then they were to create an actual model of the plane out of cardboard. On the day the class was transitioning from drawing to building the model, Julian came to school with anticipated excitement, but his teacher blocked him at the door:

Teacher: Julian, you can't enter the classroom.

Julian: What do you mean I can't enter the class? Why?

Teacher: You can't enter the classroom because we are using X-Acto knives and I don't know if you're going to stab somebody, and I don't want anyone killed on my watch.

Julian: (surprised and then frustrated): Well, then, can you just give me my drawing so I can build it at home?

Teacher: No. You can't build it at home because I won't know if you did it or not, and I won't be able to give you credit.

For the next two weeks, while Julian's peers were cutting and building their models, he wasn't allowed to attend class. At the end of the term, the teacher assigned an F for his grade.

Julian shared that this was a memorable example of his racialization, but not an isolated one. He felt these tensions in all his classes, whether it was English, math, or history. Fueled by the critical lens he was learning at home, he would challenge his teachers' Eurocentric and deficit narratives; they would tell him he was wrong, claim he didn't know what he was saying, and kick him out of class. He expressed, "I was in the process where you just can't succeed . . . so that conditioned me to believe that I wasn't intelligent, that I didn't belong [in school], and that maybe the narratives being told to me by educators were true."

Without a sense of belonging in his education, Julian got caught up with violence in his community, and in his junior year, he was shot in his neck and shoulder. These injuries solidified the narratives his teachers had of him; Julian shared that they became afraid of him and disinvested even further. It was only from the vigilance of his mother—she had badgered his counselors, signed him up, physically brought him to the SAT, and facilitated the college application process—that Julian graduated high school able to enroll in college.

Attending a Los Angeles university, he still struggled with education until he found Chicanx studies.

> If I wouldn't have taken a Chicano studies course in college, then I would have failed out. That's where the shift happened with learning; that's where the shift happened with *everything*. I went from a 1.5 GPA kid to a 3.5 GPA kid. I started to see my success in the class. I started to see my learning being valued. My work was valued. My history was valued. What I was saying in essays, in class. I was excited to go to class. Everything changed completely.

Remembering his place in education through the curriculum, pedagogy, and professors of ethnic studies, Julian began critically reflecting on his community and dreaming of the work he was setting out to do.

I knew that we lost a lot of good people because they were kicked out of schools. I know that a lot of lives would have been different if we would have had the opportunity to learn . . . . I remember talking to my brother and cousin and I would say, "I want to be a teacher. I want to go back and I'm going to change everything. I want to change it all." And they were like, "How are you going to change it all? You can't change it all." And I was like, "No, no, no. I can change it all because it's *my* neighborhood."

He began reimagining schools:

We don't have to buy into the old traditional ways of teaching. It doesn't have to be the way that it is. What if we don't have English classes and we just have Chicano literature classes? What if we don't have history classes, and we have ethnic studies classes? What if we don't have math classes and we have this other type of math? What if we bring in programs? What if when we hire new people, we make them go through this training?

And with his renewed consciousness, Julian also began reimagining his role and responsibility in his community:

I grew up in that area and I knew I was never going to shake the way people see me. Growing up I was always positioned as a leader. I led people to do bad things, but now I can come back and pay it forward and be a leader that does good things. The idea of coming back to teach was the idea of reclaiming myself, reclaiming the space, and reclaiming my future and the futures of everybody else in my neighborhood. I had the power *and* I had the responsibility to be that person.

And that's exactly what Julian did.

When he graduated college, he was hired as part of a cluster of critical educators into a new high school in his hometown, led by two Latino school leaders who were also from the community. The group of them shared a vision for reimagining and reclaiming their education, but Julian learned quickly that he and his partners in this work first needed to build trust through a demonstrated commitment and work ethic with the students, administrators, and other teachers. As Julian earned a reputation as an engaging and successful educator, he also rose to leadership roles as English department chair and Advancement Via Individual Determination (AVID) coordinator where he was able to supervise other teachers and guide them in creating culturally sustaining curricula and pedagogy.

But as Julian and his colleagues were building a different approach to school, new members were elected onto the school board who were affiliated with the hospitality industry of nearby desert resorts; they were also aligned with a predominantly white teacher union that was not from the community. The night of their first meeting, they fired over twenty-five homegrown, community-responsive administrators—from the superintendent and assistant superintendent to district coordinators, principals, and assistant principals—and replaced them with traditional school leaders that were set to reestablish the status quo stories of schooling. The school structures changed back, teachers were displaced, and much of the critical work Julian and his colleagues had accomplished was being undone. The new administrators were saying, "You're teaching propaganda to kids. You're teaching lies and hatred of white folks. You're making your students radicals."

While this dramatic shift was tough, Julian geared up for the fight. He and his peers decided that rather than trying to weave their lens within the existing structures as they had been trying to do, they were going to work directly and outwardly toward their vision. They resigned from formal school leadership roles, withdrew from programs like AVID, and began organizing with the community, alumni, students, parents, and teachers. They garnered the support of one board member, and with the momentum of the 2015 statewide ethnic studies bill (which did not pass), they were able to secure ethnic studies as a graduation requirement. The next board meeting, they got approval for the Puente Project—an initiative out of UC Berkeley that provides training and support to implement a Latinx and multicultural themed curriculum into English language arts—as a way to run ethnic studies through English courses. And then at the next election in 2016, they organized once again with the community and got all of the board members who were up for reelection unseated. The new board members replaced district administrators with people aligned with this culturally and community sustaining vision, and Alicia, Julian's mother, was hired as the new principal of the high school.

With the groundwork of their organizing and these changes, Julian and his colleagues began to realize their reimagination of their schools. He shared:

> The intent was never to have one singular ethnic studies class . . . . We wanted to completely transform education and how we deliver it to our students. We wanted them to be centered in their educational experiences. We wanted to make sure the training that teachers were getting was reflective of that. We wanted to make sure that the courses that students were able to take were going to be vastly different than what they've done a couple of years ago. So, our whole thing was about

transforming the entire education of our district, and I think now we are on that road.

At the time of our interview, the group of teachers driving this work had established eighteen unique courses and over sixty sections that are taught through the lens of ethnic studies, including Race and Gender of the United States, Chicana/o/x Literature, Statistics for Social Justice, Spanish for Culture and Identity, Danza and Culture, and Social Justice Leadership, a course that engages students in research. They have also established four honors-level weighted courses with a critical lens, and are working next on developing an environmental justice course and bringing ethnic studies and Spanish dual-language immersion programs to the elementary level. The organizing group has secured a significant budget from the district for professional development for current teachers to develop their skills, and they have changed the district hiring guidelines so that "knowledge of ethnic studies" is a preferred qualification for all future hires in all disciplines.

Much of the research guiding the establishment for ethnic studies in California schools has demonstrated its impact on student attendance, academic performance, and graduation and college-going rates.[7] Consistent with this literature, Julian's district has had similar results, with huge gains in graduation rates, and students going off to attend higher education across the University of California system. But how Julian gauges the success of their work extends beyond "student outcomes;" rather, it is that young people who attend college are returning to the region to participate in community-sustaining and community-oriented work. Julian elaborated:

> Students have always come back; I want to make that clear. But it's the intent and purpose to why they come back [that

142

has changed]. Folks working in nonprofits to deal with the infrastructure of trailer parks, looking at health issues, working with the census to make sure resources are allocated. There are alumni creating educational policy, or even teaching side by side with their teachers now. They are coming back and are serving the greater needs of the community.

Julian was born into activism, but the schools he attended and the educators within them saw his community through a deficit lens and did their best to diminish his truth and power.

It was through his mother's refusal to accept a devalued narrative of her son and the power of ethnic studies that Julian remembered his rightful place in education. He reimagined schools where young people would make sense of their lives and learn the power of their ancestors and community, and he has worked tirelessly to transform the schooling system toward that goal. And now Julian has one son attending, and another who will eventually attend, the school where their father teaches and their grandmother leads. In talking with his younger son about education, Julian reflected:

> When I was growing up, I went through thirteen years of school (counting kindergarten) and I had one or two teachers that I could really pinpoint that helped me. And think about all the teachers now through our programming, you might have the opposite. You might have one or two teachers that are going to hold you back. Your experience is going to be so concentrated with caring and transformative teachers that you are going to be able to find out how great you truly are.

Through a resistance to what is and a collective imagination of what could be, Julian worked to reclaim schools with and for his community, and he was now able to provide his sons the education generations of his family had dreamed of.

RECLAIMING EDUCATION

And who will join this standing up
and the ones who stood without sweet company
will sing and sing
back into the mountains and
if necessary
even under the sea
we are the ones we have been waiting for.

—June Jordan[8]

As discussed in chapter 1, the US system of schooling was created as a project of cultural and linguistic annihilation of Black, Indigenous, and people of Color. For generations, schools and harmful teachers have disrupted lineages of language, culture, and pride of communities of Color. Yet, as with every justice movement in our society, progress for marginalized people has been from *their* struggle, sacrifice, and resistance—from their radical imagination of a more free place, from their collective action toward realizing their dreams. As a commemoration to forty thousand women and children who protested against apartheid in South Africa in 1956, June Jordan penned the poem that ends with the stanza above and the line "we are the ones we have been waiting for." Like the freedom fighters June Jordan speaks of, as they resist racism and reclaim education, the powerful teachers of Color in this chapter are the ones they and their communities have been waiting for.[9]

From Salina's vision of relational and restorative Black scientists to Lelei's reintegration of land education and Christina's dream for students to be their own community leaders, the educators defied and redefined the boundaries of their profession as they reimagined what classrooms could be like. Ramona and Julian built upon their tools of resistance—their racial literacies from their families, communities, and ethnic studies; their communities of resistance as they built coalitions with like-minded educators and community members; and their organizing for change—to reimagine schools and districts as affirming community spaces with caring, racially and ideologically reflective teachers. As these justice-oriented teachers of Color fight to bring their history, cultural wealth, and knowledge systems into focus, they are building from their ancestors' dreams for generations to come.

6

A Path Forward

Supporting Teachers of Color

LESSONS LEARNED

As understood through the narratives of this book, the experiences of teachers of Color are complex and nuanced. We must resist the temptation to interpret them as a monolith across race, gender, geography, and professional position, yet it is also important to recognize that their experiences are interrelated. When read together, these thirty counterstories present clear lessons about how racialization operates and must be challenged within US schools.

The US educational system is interwoven with a legacy of racism, where institutions were constructed to maintain hierarchies of race, culture, and language. Although this occurred for various communities of Color in different moments and through different means, ultimately schools were designed to uphold white dominance. And those structures linger, continuing to negatively impact both students of Color *and* teachers of Color. As we saw in chapter 2, the institutional racism of schools is often layered with interpersonal manifestations of racial harm. Through narratives that include a formerly undocumented Latino teacher in Eastern

Washington, a biracial Black teacher from Minneapolis, a Pilipino teacher from California's Central Valley, a Samoan teacher in Hawai'i, an Afro-Latina Dominican teacher born and raised in the Bronx, and more, this book reveals racialized experiences that span the academic and professional trajectories of a diverse range of teachers of Color—as young people in their own K–12 education, through their respective teacher preparation programs, and across their tenure as teachers in a white-dominated profession. The racializing experiences across their lives accumulate and serve to diminish the power and gifts of teachers of Color, constructing a dominant narrative that they will never fully be welcome in schools.

As the teachers conveyed in chapter 3, the racial stress they endure battling racism is layered upon the professional stressors that all teachers face, and it takes a toll. Relentless racial harm can lead to racial battle fatigue where teachers are impacted socioemotionally, psychologically, and physiologically. Their mental and physical well-being, and sometimes even their lives, are endangered. Thus, many feel they have no choice but to leave their school or, in more dire situations, the profession altogether.

So why would a person of Color want to teach in the face of all of this? The teachers in this book reveal commitments that reach far deeper than a professional responsibility. Teachers echoed repeatedly that they had entered the teaching profession hoping to be the educators they never had, striving to create classrooms and schools that value and nurture students of Color. And they are not the first generation to feel this way: teachers of Color represent a long lineage of activists and educators fighting for the dignity of their communities. In the face of so many obstacles, these commitments have brought them to this work and continually drive them to resist. In chapter 4, we saw that the survival and resistance of teachers of Color was grounded in three tools: 1) strengthening their racial literacy to better name, navigate, and disrupt racism; 2) building communities of resistance with ideologically aligned educators, often within critical professional development spaces; and 3) organizing to collectively resist racial injustice.

While sharpening these tools has aided in the professional retention of teachers of Color, as people who have and continue to endure racism in multiple facets of their lives, resistance can also come at a cost. To expend so much energy simultaneously experiencing and fighting oppression—to be in a constant state of opposition—can leave one depleted and with little to hope for. Thus, as various scholars and activists have noted throughout time, it is important for people of Color to not only resist, but also dream beyond a state of opposition, toward a world of possibility. For many teachers of Color, this means moving past antiracist education to a vision of educational freedom, where young people of Color and their communities feel valued, empowered, whole. In chapter 5, we see how educators have taken up this call to powerfully bring their radical imagination to life, reclaiming schools to celebrate and center the epistemologies, ontologies, and power of people of Color, a process that has been healing and transformative to them as well.

INSTITUTIONAL RESPONSIBILITY

In recognizing the incredible power that teachers of Color possess to challenge and reimagine classrooms, schools, and districts, it may be tempting to rely on their strengths to remedy what is wrong with the education system. However, they did not create the inequities that exist. And while their survival and love for their community is intertwined with striving for racial justice, with such a tax to their well-being in this work, they should not be responsible for shouldering this burden. Critical Race Theory (CRT) reminds us that injustice is built into the laws, policies, and practices that govern schools. Thus, while many teachers of Color have demonstrated a capacity to brave racial harm for the sake of their communities, leaders and practitioners of teacher education, schools, and districts must be accountable to challenge racism in multifaceted ways, and create spaces that feel welcoming, safe, and responsive to marginalized people.

What Teacher Education Programs Can Do

For decades, scholars and practitioners of teacher education have pointed to the "overwhelming presence of Whiteness," the "hysterical blindness and ideologies of denial" regarding issues of race, and "the new racism," where racial oppression is subversively hidden in policies and practices that replicate inequities.[1] In a field where the majority of teacher educators and teacher candidates are white, and curriculum rarely interrogates oppression because it is structured to privilege white comfort, teacher education as it currently functions is a perfect storm for maintaining white supremacy in the education system.[2]

An important step toward disrupting this status quo is for teacher education program leaders to reflect upon and acknowledge their culpability in maintaining a politically passive, primarily white educator workforce that enacts harm. Out of financial pressure, universities frequently privilege the quantity of teacher candidates over their cultural competencies, rationalizing that it is the job of the program to shift their ideologies. But with shortened timeframes, the reduction of theory courses, and inadequate professional development for supervisors and mentor teachers, transforming the lens of teacher candidates who view communities of Color through deficits within the span of a program is often an unreasonable feat. In more recent years, a solution to fostering a more culturally responsive teaching force has been to increase its diversity. Yet, as some programs have focused on recruiting teacher candidates of Color, they have done very little to change the structures of the program; consequently, they have enlisted already minoritized educators into hostile climates not designed for their success.[3] It is important for teacher education program leaders to reflect on the demographics *and* ideological commitments of their teacher candidates, program staff, and school partners, and to consider how to establish and maintain learning environments that nurture the well-being of teacher candidates of Color.

To create teacher training where teacher candidates of Color thrive, programs must actively reduce racism and facilitate healthier racial climates where the identities, epistemologies, visions, and needs of communities of Color are respected. As a means of assessment, programs should reflect upon questions such as the following:

- In what ways do admissions processes recruit and admit teacher candidates who respect and value communities of Color?
- What policies and practices serve as barriers to the presence and well-being of teacher candidates of Color?
- How are staff and mentor teachers both equipped and developed to serve teacher candidates of Color?
- In what ways does the program establish and monitor learning environments that address racism and reflect the histories, cultures, and value systems of teacher candidates of Color?[4]

A first step toward creating a healthier environment for teacher candidates of Color within teacher education programs is to increase the racial diversity, which must include material commitments to these efforts. Thus, undergraduate education programs should consider partnering with high schools and campus summer programs that would yield diverse pipelines; graduate programs should recruit from student organizations and majors that draw students of Color; and programs at both levels should provide resources that support aspiring teachers through prerequisite exams and the high cost of tuition and assessments—known barriers to their matriculation. Next, it is also important to recognize that the racial dispositions of peers in the program also have great impact on the well-being of teachers of Color. To filter out students who may contribute to a deficit or dehumanizing culture, programs should consider "asset framing of communities of Color" a core competency or requirement for admissions.

In addition to *who* is in the program, the structures of the program must also consider the epistemologies and ontologies of communities of Color. In opposition to the individualizing culture of schooling that serves to isolate teachers of Color, teacher training should approach education through a sense of collectivism by modeling and affirming that collaborative approaches to planning, teaching, and creating change are foundational to professional success. The curriculum must also foster the racial literacy of all teacher candidates, offering them access to critical theory and readings from theorists who are Black, Indigenous, and people of Color, and explicitly strengthening their skills to navigate the racial climates of K–12 schools. Rather than constraining critical content into one "multicultural" or social foundations course, coursework across the program must strengthen teacher candidates' capacity to create humanizing, liberatory classrooms.

To realize these goals, programs must ensure that teacher education faculty and teacher mentors are racially, culturally, and linguistically diverse; have advanced racial literacies; and are ready to actively resist harm. Teacher education program leaders can invest in the development of their staff through literature circles or by funding their participation in race-focused professional development seminars. It is also important for teacher education programs to leverage institutional resources and supplement curriculum with speakers and workshops by critical scholars, model teachers of Color, and community-based partners, providing teacher candidates of Color networks of support and resources beyond their program.

Finally, in addition to proactive policies designed to support the well-being of teachers of Color, programs must also be prepared to respond to racial harm as it predictably arises. In addition to having staff who competently teach about race and racism, programs must also have policies, protocols, and established practices to directly address racial injustice within courses, in school placements, and between students and/or staff.[5]

What Schools and Districts Can Do

With increased reliance on standardized tests to measure school success and the related reward structure, US society has trended toward valuing what students produce (i.e., outcomes, achievement) over their learning or their humanity.[6] As research has demonstrated that teachers of Color have a positive impact on the academic achievement of students of Color—a group that makes up more than half of the public school student population—the interest in raising test scores has converged with an interest in diversifying the teaching force. Thus, teachers of color are often recruited into schools for the material value of their labor (i.e., how they can help schools produce better) rather than their humanistic value (their pedagogy, care, and advocacy for communities of Color).[7] It is in this archetype that teachers of Color feel commodified, struggle to realize their purpose, and end up depleted and pushed out of the profession.

As school and district leaders consider how to create healthy racial climates where teachers of Color grow, stay, succeed, and contribute to the reimagination of education, they must make key commitments. The first is an institutional responsibility to challenge racism and strive for racial justice. This cannot be a fleeting, abstract, or surface-level response to social pressure or a social moment; it must instead be substantive, concrete, and sustained.[8] Rather than relying on teachers of Color to carry race-focused work in schools, as we saw across this book, administrators must begin to recognize racial literacy as a core competency for *all* staff. This can look like adding an "asset framing of communities of Color" to hiring rubrics, providing racial literacy development for existing staff, forming compensated committees for racial justice work, and dedicating time within staff meetings to reflect upon patterns of racial inequities in policies and practices. In order for teachers of Color to not be racially isolated, this also should include strategic efforts to recruit for diversity in the teaching staff through university partnerships, as well as community-based pipeline programs such as Grow Your Own models.[9]

Alongside systemic commitments to racial justice, as schools recruit teachers of Color, it is equally important to reflect on how these educators are perceived, treated, and supported within their jobs. School leaders should consider questions such as these:

- What kinds of contributions are you expecting from teachers of Color, and how does that differ from your expectation of white teachers?
- How do you communicate your trust and value of teachers of Color? Do you listen to their insights and understandings?
- How do you invest in the growth, leadership, and visions of teachers of Color? Do you (materially) recognize their unique assets and strengths through compensation, in formal evaluations, and in leadership opportunities?

And last, the teachers in this book have shared how important racially affinity and politically aligned communities are to their growth and retention. Several teacher activist groups such as the New York Collective of Radical Educators (NYCoRE), as well as convenings such as the Institute for Teachers of Color Committed to Racial Justice (ITOC) and Free Minds Free People, have dedicated time and space for teachers of Color to meet and connect around their needs and goals. There must also be localized attempts to develop support networks and leadership skills for teachers of Color. School and district leaders should fund the attendance of teachers of Color at conferences and critical professional development spaces that align with their visions and goals in the profession. Schools and districts can also facilitate internal mentoring and network programs for teachers of Color that include mentoring, professional growth, and community building.

TEACHERS OF COLOR STANDING IN THEIR TRUTHS

> The intense isolation that manifests as an educator of Color dedicated to racial and social justice can be debilitating. Yet the joy and beauty that grows out of solidarity toward racial justice spawns the strength to carry on the work.

—Ramón, high school English teacher

Through the counterstories of this book, it is clear that justice-oriented teachers of Color have insights into the harm that students of Color experience in school. Yet they are silenced and made to feel irrational in their efforts to disrupt it. In part, this happens because schools operate through normalized systems of power and hierarchy that position students and families of Color as passive recipients to their education. Any challenge to this approach is perceived as a threat to the existing structures that so many have been socialized into. But teachers of Color must hold tightly to their truths and intuition. They must believe in their power to resist status quo stories about what schools should be and who should work there.

It is my hope that the counterstories in this book encourage teachers of Color to feel emboldened in reframing these status quo stories: So they do not quiet themselves when they are called the angry person of Color in a teacher meeting, but instead feel righteous in questioning why others do not share their anger and frustration. So they do not shrink when their pedagogy is questioned because they circumvented the textbook, but instead stand in the truth that traditional curriculum was not designed for the liberation of students of Color. So they are not scared to speak in staff meetings because peers have questioned their intelligence and those of their students, but instead know that the knowledge and insights of communities of Color are valuable and will lead to a path of reimagining schools. Standing on the shoulders of their ancestors, the teachers of Color in this book—and so many others who work in schooling systems steeped in whiteness—have endured great harm as they resist racial injustice in schools. Yet they are powerful actors in the process of reclaiming education from legacies of white supremacy, and they must be supported, appreciated, and honored as they strive to create humanizing, holistic places of learning and joy for students of Color.

NOTES

SERIES FOREWORD

1. *Brown v. Board of Education of Topeka*, 347 US 483 (1954).

FOREWORD

1. Rita Kohli, "Breaking the Cycle of Racism in the Classroom: Critical Race Reflections of Women of Color Educators" (PhD diss., University of California, Los Angeles, 2008).
2. Paulo Freire, *Pedagogy of the Oppressed* (New York: Seabury, 1970); Paulo Freire, *Education for Critical Consciousness* (New York: Seabury, 1973).
3. This may be the first time I used an asset-based methodology or what we now call a *community culture wealth framework* to work with and build on the strengths of our students and communities. See Octavio Villalpando and Daniel G. Solórzano, "The Role of Culture in College Preparation Programs: A Review of the Research Literature," in *Preparing for College: Nine Elements of Effective Outreach*, ed. William G. Tierney, Zoe B. Corwin, and Julia E. Colyar (Albany: SUNY Press, 2005), 13–28; Tara Yosso, "Whose Culture Has Capital? A Critical Race Theory Discussion of Community Cultural Wealth," *Race Ethnicity and Education* 8 (2005): 69–91; Tara J. Yosso and Daniel Solórzano, "Conceptualizing a Critical Race Theory in Sociology," in *Blackwell Companion to Social Inequalities*, ed. Mary Romero and Eric Margolis (London: Blackwell, 2005), 117–46.
4. Roach Van Allen, *Attitudes and the Art of Teaching Reading* (Washington, DC: National Education Association, 1965), https://files.eric.ed.gov/fulltext/ED038240.pdf; Roach Van Allen, "How a Language Experience Program Works" (1967), https://eric.ed.gov/?q=roach+van+allen&ft=on&id=ED012226.
5. See Daniel G. Solórzano, "Critical Race Theory's Intellectual Roots: My Email Epistolary with Derrick Bell," in *Handbook of Critical Race Theory in Education*, ed. Marvin Lynn and Adrienne D. Dixson (New York: Routledge, 2013), 48–68.
6. I continued to use variations of Freire's problem-posing pedagogy in my college classrooms. See Renée Smith-Maddox and Daniel G. Solórzano, "Using Critical Race Theory, Paulo Freire's Problem Posing Method, and Case Study Research to Confront Race and Racism in Education," *Qualitative Inquiry* 8, no. 1 (2002): 66–84; Daniel G. Solórzano, "Teaching and Social Change: Reflections on a Freirean Approach in a College Classroom," *Teaching Sociology* 17, no. 2 (1989): 218–25; Solórzano, "Critical Race Theory's Intellectual Roots"; Daniel G. Solorzano, "A

Freirean Journey from Chicana and Chicano Studies to Critical Race Theory," in *The Wiley Handbook of Paulo Freire*, ed. Carlos Alberto Torres (Hoboken, NJ: John Wiley and Sons, 2019), 417–29; Daniel Solórzano and Tara J. Yosso, "Maintaining Social Justice Hopes within Academic Realities: A Freirean Approach to Critical Race/Latcrit Pedagogy," *Denver Law Review* 78, no. 4 (2001): 595–621.

7. Patricia Hill Collins, *Black Feminist Thought: Knowledge, Consciousness, and the Politics of Empowerment*, 2nd ed. (New York: Routledge, 2000), 201, 203.

8. See Chapter 9, "Rethinking Black Women's Activism" in Collins, *Black Feminist Thought*. See also Dolores Delgado Bernal, "Grassroots Leadership Reconceptualized: Chicana Oral Histories and the 1968 East Los Angeles School Blowouts," *Frontiers: A Journal of Women Studies* 19, no. 2 (1998): 113–42; Tondra L. Loder-Jackson, *Schoolhouse Activists: African American Educators and the Long Birmingham Civil Rights Movement* (Albany: SUNY Press, 2015) ; Tondra L. Loder-Jackson, Lois McFadyen Christensen, and Hilton Kelly, "Unearthing and Bequeathing Black Feminist Legacies of *Brown* to a New Generation of Women and Girls," *Journal of Negro Education* 85, no. 3 (2016): 199–211.

9. See Philis M. Barragán Goetz, *Reading, Writing, and Revolution: Escuelitas and the Emergence of a Mexican American Identity in Texas* (Austin: University of Texas Press, 2020); Loder-Jackson, *Schoolhouse Activists*; Loder-Jackson et al., "Unearthing and Bequeathing Black Feminist Legacies of *Brown*"; Vanessa Siddle Walker, *Their Highest Potential: An African American School Community in the Segregated South* (Chapel Hill: University of North Carolina Press, 1996).

CHAPTER 1

1. Throughout this book, I use the term *of Color* when referring to the aggregate of various groups of racially minoritized people (further explanation provided in the section "Language and Labels"). I am also aware of the term *Black, Indigenous, and people of Color* (BIPOC) that is increasingly used to distinguish and recognize the unique positionalities and struggles of racialized people in the US. At times, I use this concept within the book, particularly when speaking of the aggregate of all racialized groups. I use the term *Black* when referring to people of African descent from the US and from other parts of the world. Much like how *Asian American, Indigenous,* and *Latinx* are capitalized, I capitalize these terms to honor the power and dignity of these identities. To read more about the rationale behind capitalization, see Mike Laws, "Why We Capitalize 'Black' (and not 'white')," *Columbia Journalism* Review, June 16, 2020, https://www.cjr.org/analysis/capital-b-black-styleguide.php.

2. Names in the book have been changed to protect confidentiality, unless the participant has requested to have their actual name included.

3. Personal communication, February 17, 2017.

4. Personal communication, February 17, 2017.

5. Greer, Facebook post, February 16, 2017.

6. Greer, Facebook post, February 16, 2017.

7. Yukari Takimoto Amos, *Latina Bilingual Education Teachers: Examining Structural Racism in Schools* (New York: Routledge, 2018); Rita Kohli, "Behind School Doors: The Impact of Hostile Racial Climates on Urban Teachers of Color," *Urban*

Education 53, no. 3 (2018): 307–33, https://doi.org/10.1177/0042085916636653; Xue Lan Rong and Judith Preissle, "The Continuing Decline in Asian American Teachers," *American Educational Research Journal* 34, no. 2 (1997): 267–93.

8. *Brown v. Board of Education of Topeka*, 347 US 483 (1954).

9. Michael Fultz, "The Displacement of Black Educators Post-*Brown*: An Overview and Analysis," *History of Education Quarterly* 44, no. 1 (2004): 11–45.

10. Mildred J. Hudson and Barbara J. Holmes, "Missing Teachers, Impaired Communities: The Unanticipated Consequences of *Brown v. Board of Education* on the African American Teaching Force at the Precollegiate Level," *Journal of Negro Education* 63, no. 3 (1994): 388–93.

11. National Center for Education Statistics, 2020, http://nces.ed.gov.

12. Hua-Yu Sebastian Cherng and Peter F. Halpin, "The Importance of Minority Teachers: Student Perceptions of Minority Versus White Teachers," *Educational Researcher* 45, no. 7 (2016): 407–20; US Department of Education, *The State of Racial Diversity in the Educator Workforce* (Washington, DC: Office of Planning, Evaluation and Policy, Development, 2016), https://www2.ed.gov/rschstat/eval/highered/racial-diversity/state-racial-diversity-workforce.pdf.

13. Richard M. Ingersoll and Henry May, "The Magnitude, Destinations, and Determinants of Mathematics and Science Teacher Turnover," *Educational Evaluation and Policy Analysis* 34, no. 4 (2012): 435–64; Desiree Carver-Thomas and Linda Darling-Hammond, "The Trouble with Teacher Turnover: How Teacher Attrition Affects Students and Schools," *Education Policy Analysis Archives* 27 (2019): 36.

14. Betty Achinstein and Rodney T. Ogawa, *Change(d) Agents: New Teachers of Color in Urban Schools* (New York: Teachers College Press, 2011); Betty Achinstein et al., "Retaining Teachers of Color: A Pressing Problem and a Potential Strategy for 'Hard-to-Staff' Schools," *Review of Educational Research* 80, no. 1 (2010): 71–107; Carver-Thomas and Darling-Hammond, "The Trouble with Teacher Turnover," 36.

15. Amos, *Latina Bilingual Education Teachers*; Abiola A. Farinde, Ayana Allen, and Chance W. Lewis, "Retaining Black Teachers: An Examination of Black Female Teachers' Intentions to Remain in K–12 Classrooms," *Equity & Excellence in Education* 49, no. 1 (2016): 115–27; Abiola Farinde-Wu et al., "The Urban Factor: Examining Why Black Female Educators Teach in Under-Resourced, Urban Schools," in *Black Female Teachers: Diversifying the United States' Teacher Workforce*, ed. Abiola Farinde-Wu, Ayana Allen-Handy, and Chance W. Lewis (Bingley, West Yorkshire, England: Emerald Publishing Limited, 2017), 73–92.

16. Kohli, "Behind School Doors."

17. Daniel G. Solórzano, Walter R. Allen, and Grace Carroll, "A Case Study of Racial Microaggressions and Campus Racial Climate at the University of California, Berkeley," *UCLA Chicano/Latino Law Review* 23 (2002): 15–111.

18. Cheryl Harris, "Whiteness as Property," *Harvard Law Review* 106, no. 8 (June 1993): 1707–91.

19. Joel Spring, *The American School, 1642–1993* (New York: McGraw Hill, 1994).

20. Derrick Bell, *Silent Covenants: Brown v. Board of Education and the Unfulfilled Hopes for Racial Reform* (New York: Oxford University Press, 2004); James C. Jupp, Theodorea Regina Berry, and Timothy J. Lesmire, "Second-Wave White Teacher Identity Studies: A Review of White Teacher Identity Literatures from 2004 through 2014,"

Review of Educational Research 86, no. 4 (2016): 1151–91; Maenette K.P.A. Benham and Ronald H. Heck, *Culture and Educational Policy in Hawai'i: The Silencing of Native Voices* (New York: Routledge, 2013); Charles M. Wollenberg, "'Yellow Peril' in the Schools," in *The Asian American Educational Experience*, ed. Don T. Nakanishi and Tina Yamano Nishida (New York: Routledge, 1995), 3–12.

21. US Department of Education, *The State of Racial Diversity in the Educator Workforce*.

22. US Census Bureau, 2010.

23. Jupp et al., "Second-Wave White Teacher Identity Studies"; Harriet R. Tenenbaum and Martin D. Ruck, "Are Teachers' Expectations Different for Racial Minority than for European American Students? A Meta-Analysis," *Journal of Educational Psychology* 99, no. 2 (2007): 253–73; Richard R. Valencia, *The Evolution of Deficit Thinking: Educational Thought and Practice* (New York: Routledge, 2012); Connie Wun, "Unaccounted Foundations: Black Girls, Anti-Black Racism, and Punishment in Schools," *Critical Sociology* 42, no. 4–5 (2016): 737–50.

24. Prentice T. Chandler, "Blinded by the White: Social Studies and Raceless Pedagogies," *Journal of Educational Thought* 43, no. 3 (2009): 259–88; Laurie Cooper Stoll, "Constructing the Color-Blind Classroom: Teachers' Perspectives on Race and Schooling," *Race, Ethnicity & Education* 17, no. 5 (2014): 688–705.

25. Nora E. Hyland, "Being a Good Teacher of Black Students? White Teachers and Unintentional Racism," *Curriculum Inquiry* 35, no. 4 (2005): 429–59; Sabina E. Vaught and Angelina E. Castagno, "'I Don't Think I'm A Racist': Critical Race Theory, Teacher Attitudes, and Structural Racism," *Race, Ethnicity & Education* 11, no. 2 (2008): 95–113; Evelyn Y. Young, "The Four Personae of Racism: Educators' (Mis)Understanding of Individual vs. Systemic Racism," *Urban Education* 46, no. 6 (2011): 1433–60; Jennifer Buehler, "'There's a Problem, and We've Got to Face It': How Staff Members Wrestled with Race in an Urban High School," *Race Ethnicity and Education* 16, no. 5 (2013): 629–52.

26. Yukari Takimoto Amos, "Teacher Dispositions for Cultural Competence: How Should We Prepare White Teacher Candidates for More Responsibility?" *Action in Teacher Education* 33, no. 5–6 (2011): 485, doi:10.1080/01626620.2011.627037.

27. Derrick Bell, *Faces at the Bottom of the Well: The Permanence of Racism* (New York: Basic Books, 2008); bell hooks, *Salvation: Black People and Love* (New York: William Morrow, 2001); Ashley N. Woodson and Amber Pabon, "'I'm None of the Above': Exploring Themes of Heteropatriarchy in the Life Histories of Black Male Educators," *Equity & Excellence in Education* 49, no. 1 (2016): 57–71.

28. Anne Ruggles Gere, "Indian Heart/White Man's Head: Native-American Teachers in Indian Schools, 1880–1930," *History of Education Quarterly* 45, no. 1 (2005): 38–65.

29. Gere, "Indian Heart/White Man's Head," 47.

30. Zevi Gutfreund, "Immigrant Education and Race: Alternative Approaches to 'Americanization' in Los Angeles, 1910–1940," *History of Education Quarterly* 57, no. 1 (2017): 1–38.

31. Vanessa Siddle Walker, *Their Highest Potential: An African American School Community in the Segregated South* (Chapel Hill: University of North Carolina Press, 1996).

32. Siddle Walker, *Their Highest Potential*, 3.

33. hooks, *Salvation*; Siddle-Walker, *Their Highest Potential*.

34. bell hooks, *Killing Rage: Ending Racism* (New York: Henry Holt and Company, 1996).

35. William Sturkey, "'I Want to Become a Part of History': Freedom Summer, Freedom Schools, and the Freedom News," *Journal of African American History* 95, no. 3–4 (2010): 348–68.

36. D. Contreras, *Daily Sundial*, February 21, 1975.

37. Rong and Preissle, "The Continuing Decline in Asian American Teachers"; June A. Gordon, "Why Students of Color Are Not Entering Teaching: Reflections from Minority Teachers," *Journal of Teacher Education* 45, no. 5 (1994): 346–53; Martin Haberman, "More Minority Teachers," *Phi Delta Kappan* 70, no. 10 (1989): 771–6; B. Merino and R. Quintanar, *The Recruitment of Minority Students into Teaching Careers: A Status Report of Effective Approaches* (Boulder: Far West Regional Holmes Group, University of Colorado, 1988); Zhixin Su, "Why Teach: Profiles and Entry Perspectives of Minority Students as Becoming Teachers," *Journal of Research and Development in Education* 29, no. 3 (1996): 117–33; Zhixin Su, "Teaching as a Profession and as a Career: Minority Candidates' Perspectives," *Teaching and Teacher Education* 13, no. 3 (1997): 325–40.

38. Achinstein and Ogawa, *Change(d) Agents*; Anna María Villegas and Jacqueline Jordan Irvine, "Diversifying the Teaching Force: An Examination of Major Arguments," *Urban Review* 42, no. 3 (2010): 175–92; Anthony L. Brown, "'O Brotha Where Art Thou?': Examining the Ideological Discourses of African American Male Teachers Working with African American Male Students," *Race, Ethnicity and Education* 12, no. 4 (2009): 473–93; Christine E. Sleeter, "Preparing Teachers for Culturally Diverse Schools: Research and the Overwhelming Presence of Whiteness," *Journal of Teacher Education* 52, no. 2 (2001): 94–106; Evelyn Marino Weisman and Laurie E. Hansen, "Student Teaching in Urban and Suburban Schools: Perspectives of Latino Preservice Teachers," *Urban Education* 43, no. 6 (2008): 653–70; Mary Louise Gomez and Terri L. Rodriguez, "Imagining the Knowledge, Strengths, and Skills of a Latina Prospective Teacher," *Teacher Education Quarterly* 38, no. 1 (2011): 127–46; Colleen M. Eddy and Donald Easton-Brooks, "Ethnic Matching, School Placement, and Mathematics Achievement of African American Students from Kindergarten through Fifth Grade," *Urban Education* 46, no. 6 (2011): 1280–99; Marilynne Boyle-Baise and Christine E. Sleeter, "Community Service Learning for Multicultural Teacher Education," *Educational Foundations* 14, no. 2 (2000): 33–50.

39. Gomez and Rodriguez, "Imagining the Knowledge, Strengths, and Skills"; Rita Kohli, "Critical Race Reflections: Valuing the Experiences of Teachers of Color in Teacher Education," *Race Ethnicity and Education* 12, no. 2 (2009): 235–51; Reitumetse Obakang Mabokela and Jean A. Madsen, "African American Teachers in Suburban Desegregated Schools: Intergroup Differences and the Impact of Performance Pressures," *Teachers College Record* 109, no. 5 (2007): 1171–1206.

40. Robert A. Smith, "Horatio Alger Lives in Brooklyn: Extra Family Support, Intrafamily Dynamics, and Socially Neutral Operating Identities in Exceptional Mobility Among Children of Mexican Immigrants," *Annals of the American Academy of Political and Social Science* 620, no. 1 (2008): 270–90; Vivian S. Louie, *Keeping the Immigrant Bargain: The Costs and Rewards of Success in America* (New York: Russell Sage Foundation, 2012).

41. Constance A. Lindsay and Cassandra M. Hart, "Teacher Race and School Discipline: Are Students Suspended Less Often When They Have a Teacher of the Same Race?" *Education Next* 17, no. 1 (2017): 72–9.

42. National Center for Educational Statistics, 2020, https://nces.ed.gov/programs/coe/indicator_clr.asp.

43. Jason G. Irizarry, "Home Growing Teachers of Color: Lessons Learned from a Town-Gown Partnership," *Teacher Education Quarterly* 34, no. 4 (2007): 87–102; Kam Fui Lau, Evelyn B. Dandy, and Lorrie Hoffman, "The Pathways Program: A Model for Increasing the Number of Teachers of Color," *Teacher Education Quarterly* 34, no. 4 (2007): 27–40; Karen Sakash and Victoria Chou, "Increasing the Supply of Latino Bilingual Teachers for the Chicago Public Schools," *Teacher Education Quarterly* 34, no. 4 (2007): 41–52.

44. Conra D. Gist, Margarita Bianco, and Marvin Lynn, "Examining Grow Your Own Programs Across the Teacher Development Continuum: Mining Research on Teachers of Color and Nontraditional Educator Pipelines," *Journal of Teacher Education* 70, no. 1 (2019): 13–25.

45. Cheryl E. Matias and Daniel D. Liou, "Tending to the Heart of Communities of Color: Toward Critical Race Teacher Activism," *Urban Education* 50, no. 5 (2015): 601–25, doi:10.1177/0042085913519338; Conra D. Gist, "Culturally Responsive Pedagogy for Teachers of Color," *The New Educator* 13, no. 3 (2017): 288–303.

46. Yukari Takimoto Amos, "'They Don't Want To Get It!' Interaction Between Minority and White Pre-Service Teachers in a Multicultural Education Class," *Multicultural Education*, 17, no. 4 (2010): 31–7; Marcelle Haddix, "No Longer on the Margins: Researching the Hybrid Literate Identities of Black and Latina Preservice Teachers," *Research in the Teaching of English* 45, no. 2 (2010): 97–123.

47. Rachel Endo, "From Unconscious Deficit Views to Affirmation of Linguistic Varieties in the Classroom: White Preservice Teachers on Building Critical Self-Awareness about Linguicism's Causes and Consequences," *Multicultural Perspectives* 17, no. 4 (2015): 207–14; Kohli, "Behind School Doors"; Yukari Takimoto Amos, "Wanted and Used: Latina Bilingual Education Teachers at Public Schools," *Equity & Excellence in Education* 49, no. 1 (2016): 41–56; Woodson and Pabon, "I'm None of the Above."

48. Rita Kohli and Marcos Pizarro, "Fighting to Educate Our Own: Teachers of Color, Relational Accountability, and the Struggle for Racial Justice," *Equity & Excellence in Education* 49, no. 1 (2016): 72–84.

49. Gloria Ladson-Billings, "Just What Is Critical Race Theory and What's It Doing in a Nice Field Like Education?" *International Journal of Qualitative Studies in Education* 11, no. 1 (1998): 7–24, doi:10.1080/095183998236863; Daniel G. Solorzano, "Images and Words That Wound: Critical Race Theory, Racial Stereotyping, and Teacher Education," *Teacher Education Quarterly* 24, no. 3 (1997): 5–19.

50. Solorzano, "Images and Words That Wound," 8.

51. Gloria Ladson-Billings, "From the Achievement Gap to the Education Debt: Understanding Achievement in US Schools," *Educational Researcher* 35, no. 7 (2006): 3–12.

52. María C. Ledesma and Dolores Calderón, "Critical Race Theory in Education: A Review of Past Literature and a Look to the Future," *Qualitative Inquiry* 21, no. 3

(2015): 206–22, doi:10.1177/1077800414557825; Uma M. Jayakumar et al., "Racial Privilege in the Professoriate: An Exploration of Campus Climate, Retention, and Satisfaction," *Journal of Higher Education* 80, no. 5 (2009): 538–63.

53. Derrick Bell, *Faces at the Bottom of the Well: The Permanence of Racism* (New York: Basic Books, 2008).

54. Kohli, "Critical Race Reflections."

55. Kohli, "Behind School Doors"; Kohli and Pizarro, "Fighting to Educate Our Own"; Pizarro and Kohli, "I Stopped Sleeping."

56. Rita Kohli et al., "A Way of Being: Women of Color Educators and Their Ongoing Commitments to Critical Consciousness," *Teaching and Teacher Education* 82 (2019): 24–32; Rita Kohli, "Lessons for Teacher Education: The Role of Critical Professional Development in Teacher of Color Retention," *Journal of Teacher Education* 70, no. 1 (2019): 39–50.

57. For this book, I synthesized and reanalyzed data I had previously collected from qualitative questionnaires, interviews, focus groups, and digital narratives in three research studies with justice-oriented teachers of Color to understand key patterns about their racialized experiences from their own K–12 education through their tenure as K–12 teachers. To learn more about how the data was collected for those studies, please see the articles referenced in endnotes 54, 55, and 56. Based on emergent themes (racialization, impact of racism, resistance, and reimagination), I planned out the organizational structure of the book. I then went back to the data to identify key teachers of Color that had compelling experiences related to the particular themes. I invited those teachers to participate in additional in-depth interviews to further explore their academic and professional trajectories. For the twenty-five teachers who agreed to participate, we scheduled one- to two-hour virtual Zoom meetings, which I recorded using an iPhone Voice Memo app and stored on a password-protected computer. I then transcribed the interviews, reviewed the data from each teacher's interview alongside the data I had previously collected with them, and built a counterstory. There is one counterstory that was written solely from a new interview with a teacher referred to me through the recommendation of a colleague, and there are five counterstories that were written with data from previous studies alone. Dependent on current contact information, I was able to solicit feedback on the narratives from twenty-eight of the thirty teacher participants to ensure the counterstories are reflective of their experiences and understandings.

58. While storytelling has been a pedagogical tool of many communities of Color around the world for generations, the concept of counterstories and its application to academic scholarship has its origins in CRT starting with Derrick Bell, *Faces at the Bottom of the Well: The Permanence of Racism* (New York: Basic Books, 1992) and Richard Delgado, *The Rodrigo Chronicles* (New York: New York University Press, 1995). It also has roots in education research with Daniel G. Solórzano and Tara J. Yosso, "Critical Race and LatCrit Theory and Method: Counter-storytelling," *International Journal of Qualitative Studies in Education* 14, no. 4 (2001): 471–95; and Tara J. Yosso, "Whose Culture Has Capital? A Critical Race Theory Discussion of Community Cultural Wealth," *Race, Ethnicity and Education* 8, no. 1 (2005): 69–91, doi:10.1080/1361332052000341006.

59. H. Richard Milner IV and Tyrone C. Howard, "Counter-Narrative as Method: Race, Policy and Research for Teacher Education," *Race, Ethnicity and Education* 16, no. 4 (2013): 542.

60. A big thanks to Dr. Leigh Patel for her dialogue and collaborative thinking on the notion of how people assert agency as they "make homes" in their racial categories.

61. To read more about the complexity of the term *people of Color*, see E. Tammy Kim, "The Perils of 'People of Color,'" *New Yorker*, July 29, 2020, https://www.newyorker .com/news/annals-of-activism/the-perils-of-people-of-color.

62. See Shereen Marisol Meraji, "'Hispanic,' 'Latino,' or 'Latinx'? Survey Says. . .," NPR.org, August 11, 2020, https://www.npr.org/sections/codeswitch/2020/08/11/901398248 /hispanic-latino-or-latinx-survey-says; Raul A. Reyes, "Is the Term Latinx Catching On? A New Report Takes a Look," NBCNews.com, August 11, 2020, https://www .nbcnews.com/news/latino/term-latinx-catching-new-report-takes-look-n1236344.

63. Bell, *Faces at the Bottom of the Well*.

CHAPTER 2

1. Frances Kai-Hwa Wang, "No Charges for Ahmed Mohamed, Teen Arrested After Bringing Homemade Clock to School," NBC News, September 17, 2015.

2. Dean Obeidallah, "Anti-Muslim School Bullying: Sometimes, It's Even the Teachers Doing It," Daily Beast, April 13, 2017, https://www.thedailybeast.com /anti-muslim-school-bullying-sometimes-its-even-the-teachers-doing-it.

3. Debbie Truong, "Group Calls on Virginia School District to Protect Student Who Accused Teacher of Pulling Hijab," *Washington Post*, November 22, 2017, https:// www.washingtonpost.com/news/education/wp/2017/11/22/group-calls-on-virginia -school-district-to-protect-student-who-accused-teacher-of-pulling-hijab/.

4. Southern Poverty Law Center, "The Trump Effect: The Impact of the 2016 Presidential Election on Our Nation's Schools," SPLCenter.org, 2016, https://www.splcenter .org/20161128/trump-effect-impact-2016-presidential-election-our-nations-schools.

5. Donald Easton-Brooks, Chance W. Lewis, and Yubo Zhang, "Ethnic-Matching: The Influence of African American Teachers on the Reading Scores of African American Students," *National Journal of Urban Education & Practice* 3, no. 1 (2010): 230–43; Constance A. Lindsay and Cassandra M. Hart, "Teacher Race and School Discipline: Are Students Suspended Less Often When They Have a Teacher of the Same Race?" *Education Next* 17, no. 1 (2017): 72–9.

6. Mary Louise Gomez and Terri L. Rodriguez, "Imagining the Knowledge, Strengths, and Skills of a Latina Prospective Teacher," *Teacher Education Quarterly* 38, no. 1 (2011): 127–46.

7. Sharon Noguchi, "San Jose: Muslim Teacher Wearing Head Scarf Repeatedly Bullied by Students," *Mercury News*, November 24, 2017, https://www.mercu- rynews.com/2017/11/24/san-jose-muslim-teacher-wearing-head-scarf-repeatedly- bullied-by-students/.

8. "New racism" is a concept that refers to a more covert and hidden racism that has replaced the overt discriminatory policies of the past in maintaining racial hierarchies of white dominance. For more on this subject, see Eduardo Bonilla-Silva, "'New Racism,' Color-Blind Racism, and the Future of Whiteness in America," in *White Out: The Continuing Significance of Racism*, ed. Ashley W. Doane and

Eduardo Bonilla-Silva (New York: Routledge, 2003), 271–84. Or Rita Kohli, Marcos Pizarro, and Arturo Nevárez, "The 'New Racism' of K–12 Schools: Centering Critical Research on Racism," *Review of Research in Education* 41, no. 1 (2017): 182–202. Also see Richard R. Valencia, *Dismantling Contemporary Deficit Thinking: Educational Thought and Practice* (New York: Routledge, 2010); Lindsay Pérez Huber and Daniel G. Solorzano, "Racial Microaggressions as a Tool for Critical Race Research," *Race Ethnicity and Education* 18, no. 3 (2015): 297–320.

9. Rita Kohli, Nallely Arteaga, and Elexia R. McGovern, "'Compliments' and 'Jokes': Unpacking Racial Microaggressions in the K–12 Classroom," in *Microaggression Theory: Influence and Implications*, ed. Gina C. Torino et al. (Hoboken, NJ: John Wiley & Sons, 2018), 276–90.

10. Rita Kohli, "Unpacking Internalized Racism: Teachers of Color Striving for Racially Just Classrooms," *Race Ethnicity and Education* 17, no. 3 (2014): 378.

11. Valencia, *Dismantling Contemporary Deficit Thinking*.

12. Lindsay Pérez Huber et al., *Still Falling Through The Cracks: Revisiting the Latina/o Education Pipeline*, CSRC Research Report No. 19 (Los Angeles: UCLA Chicano Studies Research Center, 2015).

13. American Association of Colleges for Teacher Education, *Education Students and Diversity: A National Portrait* (Washington DC: American Association of Colleges for Teacher Education, 2019.); King & Hampel, *Colleges of Education: A National Portrait*. (Washington DC: American Association of Colleges for Teacher Education, 2018).

14. Marilyn Cochran-Smith et al., "Critiquing Teacher Preparation Research: An Overview of the Field, Part II," *Journal of Teacher Education* 66, no. 2 (2015): 109–21.

15. Beverly E. Cross, "New Racism, Reformed Teacher Education, and the Same Ole' Oppression," *Educational Studies* 38, no. 3 (2005): 263–74, https://doi.org/10.1207/s15326993es3803_6.

16. Yukari Takimoto Amos, "They Don't Want to Get It! Interaction Between Minority and White Pre-Service Teachers in a Multicultural Education Class," *Multicultural Education* 17, no. 4 (2010): 31–7.

17. Christine E. Sleeter, "Critical Race Theory and the Whiteness of Teacher Education," *Urban Education* 52, no. 2 (2017): 155–69.

18. Emery Petchauer and Lynnette Mawhinney, *Teacher Education Across Minority-Serving Institutions: Programs, Policies, and Social Justice* (New Brunswick, NJ: Rutgers University Press, 2017).

19. Yukari Takimoto Amos, *Latina Bilingual Education Teachers: Examining Structural Racism in Schools* (New York: Routledge, 2018).

20. US Census Bureau, 2010.

21. Richard R. Valencia, "'Mexican Americans Don't Value Education!' On the Basis of the Myth, Mythmaking, and Debunking," *Journal of Latinos and Education* 1, no. 2 (2002): 81–103.

22. Committee of Graduate School of Education, University of Nebraska, The Rural Teacher of Nebraska, Bureau of Education, Bulletin 1919, No. 20 (Washington, DC: GPO, 1919), 27–28.

23. Wayne Au, *Unequal by Design: High-Stakes Testing and the Standardization of Inequality* (New York: Routledge, 2010).

24. Thomas Dee and Emily Penner, "The Causal Effects of Cultural Relevance: Evidence from an Ethnic Studies Curriculum," CEPA Working Paper No. 16-01, Stanford Center for Education Policy Analysis (2016); Donald Easton-Brooks, *Ethnic Matching: Academic Success of Students of Color* (New York: Rowman & Littlefield Publishers, 2019).

25. Derrick Bell, *Silent Covenants: Brown v. Board of Education and the Unfulfilled Hopes for Racial Reform* (New York: Oxford University Press, 2004).

26. Derrick Bell, *Faces at the Bottom of the Well: The Permanence of Racism* (New York: Basic Books, 2008).

27. I borrow from Mireles to define *racist ableism*. Building upon ableism—a system that hierarchically values people's bodies and minds based on socially constructed ideas of normalcy and intelligence—Mireles defines it as "ableism informed by racist attitudes and beliefs, oppressing and dehumanizing Black, Indigenous and People of Color (BIPOC) based on actual or perceived (or, inversely, lack of perceived) dis/ability, thereby reinforcing the relationship between whiteness and ability." Danielle Mireles, "Toward a Theory of Racist Ableism in Higher Education," presented at *Political Economies of Higher Education* session at the meeting of Critical Race Studies in Education Association, Los Angeles, CA, May 2019.

28. Civil Rights Data Collection, 2017, https://ocrdata.ed.gov/.

29. Rita Kohli, "Behind School Doors: The Impact of Hostile Racial Climates on Urban Teachers of Color," *Urban Education* 53, no. 3 (2018): 307–33, https://doi .org/10.1177/0042085916636653.

30. US Department of Education, *State of Racial Diversity*.

31. MEChA is an organization that seeks to promote Chicanx unity and empowerment through political action. Originally with Chicano, and then Chican@, at the 2016 National MEChA Conference in Tucson, Arizona, students voted to change the organization's title to *Movimiento Estudiantil Chicanx de Aztlán*. In April 2019, to be more responsive to Central American and Indigenous Latina/o/x students and the changing demographics of the organization, student leaders voted to drop *Chicanx* and *Aztlán* from the group name. These changes have been debated intergenerationally within the broader MEChA community and alumni.

32. Rita Kohli and Marcos Pizarro, "Fighting to Educate Our Own: Teachers of Color, Relational Accountability, and the Struggle for Racial Justice," *Equity & Excellence in Education* 49, no. 1 (2016): 72–84.

CHAPTER 3

1. Rita Kohli, Nallely Arteaga, and Elexia R. McGovern, "'Compliments' and 'Jokes': Unpacking Racial Microaggressions in the K–12 Classroom," in *Microaggression Theory: Influence and Implications*, ed. Gina C. Torino et al. (Hoboken, NJ: John Wiley & Sons, 2018), 276–90.

2. Frantz Fanon, *Black Skin, White Masks* (New York: Grove Press, 1952), 9.

3. *Unnatural Causes*, produced by Larry Adelman and Llewellyn M. Smith (San Francisco: California Newsreel, 2009), DVD, https://unnaturalcauses.org/about_the _series.php; William A. Smith, "Black Faculty Coping with Racial Battle Fatigue: The Campus Racial Climate in a Post-Civil Rights Era," in *A Long Way to Go:*

Conversations About Race by African American Faculty and Graduate Students, ed. Darrell Cleveland (New York: Peter Lang, 2004), 171–90.

4. *State of America's Schools: The Path to Winning Again in Education* (Washington, DC: Gallup, 2014).

5. Keith C. Herman, Jal'et Hickmon-Rosa, and Wendy M. Reinke, "Empirically Derived Profiles of Teacher Stress, Burnout, Self-Efficacy, and Coping and Associated Student Outcomes," *Journal of Positive Behavior Interventions* 20, no. 2 (2018): 90–100.

6. Robert T. Carter, "Race-based Traumatic Stress," *Psychiatric Times* 23, no. 14 (2006): 37.

7. Riana Elyse Anderson et al., "EMBRacing Racial Stress and Trauma: Preliminary Feasibility and Coping Responses of a Racial Socialization Intervention," *Journal of Black Psychology* 44, no. 1 (2018): 25–46.

8. William A. Smith, "Toward an Understanding of Misandric Microaggressions and Racial Battle Fatigue Among African Americans in Historically White Institutions," in *The State of the African American Male*, ed. Eboni M. Zamani-Gallaher and Vernon C. Polite (East Lansing: Michigan State University Press, 2010), 265–77.

9. William A. Smith, Tara J. Yosso, and Daniel Solorzano, "Challenging Racial Battle Fatigue on Historically White Campuses: A Critical Race Examination of Race-Related Stress," in *Faculty of Color Teaching in Predominantly White Colleges and Universities*, ed. Christine Stanley (New York: Anker Publishing Company, 2006), 301.

10. Marcos Pizarro and Rita Kohli, "'I Stopped Sleeping': Teachers of Color and the Impact of Racial Battle Fatigue," *Urban Education* 55, no. 7 (2020): 967–91.

11. Shawn Wilson, *Research Is Ceremony: Indigenous Research Methods* (Halifax, Nova Scotia: Fernwood Publishing, 2008).

12. Wilson, *Research Is Ceremony*, 77.

13. Kohli and Pizarro adapt Wilson's framework to frame the relational accountability that justice-oriented and community-oriented teachers of Color feel in "Fighting to Educate Our Own: Teachers of Color, Relational Accountability and the Struggle for Racial Justice," *Equity and Excellence in Education* 49, no. 1 (2016): 72–84.

14. Desiree Carver-Thomas and Linda Darling-Hammond, "The Trouble with Teacher Turnover: How Teacher Attrition Affects Students and Schools," *Education Policy Analysis Archives* 27 (2019): 36.

15. Rita Kohli, "Lessons for Teacher Education: The Role of Critical Professional Development in Teacher of Color Retention," *Journal of Teacher Education* 70, no. 1 (2019): 7.

16. A compassionate approach to intervening on someone's problematic behavior while maintaining a sense of community.

17. I represent the language of the teachers of Color I interviewed as they said it, which includes the repeated use of the word *crazy*. I understand how difficult it can be to put emotions into words, and I honor the intensity of their struggle. I also feel a responsibility to complicate the use of this word, which, when used by those without mental illness, can create harm for those with mental health struggles. Thus, I also offer more precise words to describe the feeling, such as *irrational* or *illogical*. See Jennifer Kesler, "Replacing 'Crazy' for Ableism and Preciseness of Language," Feb-

ruary 10, 2011, https://web.archive.org/web/20110616134846/http://whatprivilege
.com/replacing-crazy-for-ableism-and-preciseness-of-language/.

18. I build upon Marx to describe the commodification of teachers of Color. See Karl
Marx, *Capital: Volume 1* (Moscow: Progress Press, 1867) in Kohli, "Behind School
Doors."

19. Pizarro and Kohli, "I Stopped Sleeping," 19.

CHAPTER 4

1. Lani Guinier, "From Racial Liberalism to Racial Literacy: *Brown v. Board of Education* and the Interest-Divergence Dilemma," *Journal of American History* 91, no. 1
(2004): 100.

2. For more detail on the application of racial literacy in the field of education, see
Rebecca Rogers and Melissa Mosley Wetzel, "A Critical Discourse Analysis of Racial
Literacy in Teacher Education," *Linguistics and Education* 19, no. 2 (2008): 107–31;
Yolanda Sealey-Ruiz, "Dismantling the School-to-Prison Pipeline Through Racial
Literacy Development," *Journal of Curriculum and Pedagogy* 8, no. 2 (2011): 116–20;
Allison Skerrett, "English Teachers' Racial Literacy Knowledge and Practice," *Race,
Ethnicity and Education* 14, no. 3 (2011): 313–30.

3. Rita Kohli et al., "A Way of Being: Women of Color Educators and Their Ongoing Commitments to Critical Consciousness," *Teaching and Teacher Education* 82
(2019): 27.

4. Kohli et al., "A Way of Being," 27.

5. Alternative schools, also referred to as *alternative education*, are a context for students
whose needs are not being met in a traditional educational setting. These schools
often serve students who benefit from an altered school structure or need additional
supports.

6. Rita Kohli, "Lessons for Teacher Education: The Role of Critical Professional Development in Teacher of Color Retention," *Journal of Teacher Education* 70, no. 1
(2019): 39–50.

7. Kohli, "Lessons for Teacher Education," 39.

8. Adapted from Marcos Pizarro and Rita Kohli, "'I Stopped Sleeping': Teachers of
Color and the Impact of Racial Battle Fatigue," *Urban Education* 55, no. 7 (2018):
967–91. I reflect the narratives of Liza by representing her language accurately, and
understand how difficult it can be to put emotions into words. Critical dis/ability
scholars have also complicated the use of the term *crazy* as an ableist word that can
create harm for people with mental illness. In the case of Liza, who experienced
mental health concerns, this word may hold a different meaning, but in many cases,
a more precise word or phrase can describe the feeling, such as *irrational, illogical,
unintelligent,* or *not making sense.*

9. bell hooks, *Yearning: Race, Gender, and Cultural Politics* (New York: Routledge,
2014), 213.

10. See www.instituteforteachersofcolor.org.

11. *Racial capitalism* is "the process of deriving social and economic value from racial
identity," such as when the few people of Color at a predominantly white institution
are included in the promotional materials to promote a face of diversity. To learn

more, see Nancy Leong, "Racial Capitalism," *Harvard Law Review* 126 (2012): 2151–2226. *Neoliberalism* refers to market-oriented reform policies that reduce the influence of the state through privatization.

12. *Do now* refers to brief warm-up activities that teachers use to engage students at the start of a lesson.

13. Rita Kohli et al., "Critical Professional Development: Centering the Social Justice Needs of Teachers," *International Journal of Critical Pedagogy* 6, no. 2 (2012): 7.

14. Micia Mosely, "The Black Teacher Project: How Racial Affinity Professional Development Sustains Black Teachers," *Urban Review* 50, no. 2 (2018): 267–83.

15. *Filipino* is the Hispanized way of referring to both the people and the language in the Philippines. Since most languages indigenous to the Phillipines do not have the "F" sound, the use of the term *Pilipino* is also an act of defiance to European hegemony. See Tracy Lachica Buenavista, "Model (Undocumented) Minorities and 'Illegal' Immigrants: Centering Asian Americans and US Carcerality in Undocumented Student Discourse," *Race Ethnicity and Education* 21, no. 1 (2018): 78–91.

16. To read more about Pin@y Educational Partnership, see http://www.pepsf.org/origins-of-pep.html.

17. Pizarro and Kohli, "I Stopped Sleeping," 14.

18. ICE stands for Immigration and Customs Enforcement.

CHAPTER 5

1. AnaLouise Keating, "Transforming Status-Quo Stories," *Education and Hope in Troubled Times: Visions of Change for Our Children's World* (New York: Routledge, 2009), 34.

2. Robin G. D. Kelly, *Freedom Dreams: The Black Radical Imagination* (Boston: Beacon Press, 2002), 2–3.

3. Maisha T. Winn, *Justice on Both Sides: Transforming Education Through Restorative Justice* (Cambridge, MA: Harvard Education Press, 2018).

4. You can access the full framework at: Alexis Patterson and Salina Gray, "Teaching to Transform:(W) holistic Science Pedagogy," *Theory Into Practice* 58, no. 4 (2019): 328–337.

5. Julio Cammarota and Michelle Fine, eds., *Revolutionizing Education: Youth Participatory Action Research in Motion* (New York: Routledge, 2010), vii.

6. R. Grunewald, "A Statewide Crisis: Minnesota's Educational Achievement Gap," 2019, *Federal Reserve Bank of Minneapolis*; Erin Hinrichs, "Report Dives into Why Increasing Teacher Diversity in Minneapolis is So Difficult," *Minnesota Post*, March 1, 2018, https://www.minnpost.com/education/2018/03/report-dives-why-increasing-teacher-diversity-minneapolis-so-difficult/.

7. Thomas Dee and Emily Penner, "The Causal Effects of Cultural Relevance: Evidence from an Ethnic Studies Curriculum. CEPA Working Paper No. 16-01," *Stanford Center for Education Policy Analysis* (2016).

8. June Jordan, "Poem for South African Women," *Passion New Poems 1977–1980* (1980).

9. The sentiment that teachers of Color are the leaders they have been waiting for was presented by Rebeca Burciaga in her 2017 Keynote for the Institute for Teachers of

Color Committed to Racial Justice; and the notion that teachers of Color are the ones they have been waiting for was presented by Leigh Patel in her 2020 Keynote for the Institute for Teachers of Color Committed to Racial Justice.

CHAPTER 6

1. Christine E. Sleeter, "Preparing Teachers for Culturally Diverse Schools: Research and the Overwhelming Presence of Whiteness," *Journal of Teacher Education* 52, no. 2 (2001): 94–106; Ricardo E. Gonsalves, "Chapter One: Hysterical Blindness and the Ideology of Denial: Preservice Teachers' Resistance to Multicultural Education," *Counterpoints* 319 (2008): 3–27; Beverly E. Cross, "New Racism, Reformed Teacher Education, and the Same Ole' Oppression," *Educational Studies* 38, no. 3 (2005): 263–74.
2. Mariana Souto-Manning, "Toward Praxically-Just Transformations: Interrupting Racism in Teacher Education," *Journal of Education for Teaching* 45, no. 1 (2019): 97–113.
3. Yukari Takimoto Amos, "They Don't Want to Get It!": Interaction Between Minority and White Pre-Service Teachers in a Multicultural Education Class," *Multicultural Education* 17, no. 4 (2010): 31–7.
4. I first presented on versions of these questions at the 2019 keynote for the California Council for Teacher Education. We have built upon these questions in a model of Healthy Racial Climate in Teacher Education, funded by the California Teacher Education Research and Improvement Network.
5. This recommendation comes from the Healthy Racial Climate in Teacher Education framework that we collectively conceptualized in Rita Kohli, Alison Dover, Uma Jayakumar, Darlene Lee, Nicholas Henning, Eddie Comeaux, Arturo Nevárez, Emma Hipolito, and Andrea Carreno Cortez, "Centering Teacher Candidates of Color: Towards a Healthy Racial Climate in Teacher," forthcoming (2021).
6. Wayne Au, *Unequal by Design: High-Stakes Testing and the Standardization of Inequality* (New York: Routledge, 2010).
7. Karl Marx, *Capital: Volume 1* (Moscow: Progress Press, 1867).
8. We witnessed a heightened racial awareness to antiblackness in 2020 in response to the state-sanctioned murder of George Floyd. Yet the broad social commitment of many organizations to standing for Black lives did not always manifest in systemic changes that lasted.
9. Conra D. Gist, Margarita Bianco, and Marvin Lynn, "Examining Grow Your Own Programs Across the Teacher Development Continuum: Mining Research on Teachers of Color and Nontraditional Educator Pipelines," *Journal of Teacher Education* 70, no. 1 (2019): 13–25.

ACKNOWLEDGMENTS

I am so thankful to the teachers whose narratives are included in this book, who trusted me to share their vulnerable moments of struggle and their powerful movements in resistance. Your tireless efforts toward liberatory education for communities of Color is inspirational, and I hope that you always remember how important your place in schools truly is.

I would like to also acknowledge my family for all their support through this process, especially my partner, John, who consistently read and talked through my writing and engaged the kids (during a pandemic) so I could work; my daughters, Asha and Anaya, who drew many book covers, listened to me read chapters aloud, and, most importantly, gave me hugs when I most needed them; and my parents, Neena and Jogindra, my brother, Sharad, and my in-laws, Ardrena and Tom, who are continually inquisitive and supportive.

A big thank you to Rich Milner and Jayne Fargnoli for including me in this significant series and always being so encouraging of my work, to Arturo Nevárez for your thoughtful comments, and to Jordan Beltran Gonzalez for your attention to detail, positivity, and incredible support throughout the process.

I am forever grateful to my brilliant mentor, Daniel Solórzano, who embodies the powerful balance of fierce racial justice warrior and compassionate, humanizing educator, and who took time and care to write a meaningful foreword. A big shout-out to my academic family, Marcos Pizarro, for thinking, dreaming, and building those dreams into reality with me for the last decade. Our collaboration has been foundational to this work and to my growth as a scholar and as a person. I must also acknowledge our ITOC community and all the wonderful, inspiring teachers—you all give me hope in the possibilities of a more just world. Another big thank you to Leigh Patel for your femtorship, deep care, and unwavering encouragement for me to see the value of my voice; and so much appreciation to my dear friends Nickie Johnson-Ahorlu, Dimpal Jain, and Adai Tefera, who have been critical thought partners and cheerleaders for this book and in life.

ABOUT THE AUTHOR

Rita Kohli is an associate professor of teaching and teacher education in the Graduate School of Education at the University of California, Riverside (UCR). Building on her experiences as an urban public middle school teacher and a teacher educator, and on her scholarly training in critical race theory, she has spent the last decade researching race, power, and in/equity in the professional experiences and well-being of teachers of Color. Committed to praxis, she is also a cofounder and codirector of the Institute for Teachers of Color Committed to Racial Justice (ITOC; http://www.instituteforteachersofcolor.org). Through ITOC, she has applied her scholarly insights to programming that supports the retention, racial literacy growth, and racial justice leadership development of teachers of Color in K–12 schools.

Kohli is also the coeditor of the book *Confronting Racism in Teacher Education: Narratives from Teacher Educators* (Routledge, 2017), and her scholarly work has been recognized through several local and national awards, including the UCR Innovator for Social Change Award, the Scholar Activist and Community Advocacy Award from the Critical Educators for Social Justice Special Interest Group of the American Educational Research Association (AERA), and the Early Career Award in Division G, Social Context of Education, also from AERA.

INDEX

standardized testing, 43, 153
status quo, within schools, 113–114
stress. *See also* racial battle fatigue
  activism and, 92
  effects of, 148
  extreme, 65–67
  racial, 61–63, 93, 108
strikes, 62, 103–106, 128
structural racism, 100–101, 107, 156
students of Color
  academic achievement of, 153–154
  activism of, 10
  African American, 47–48
  demographics of, 12, 34–35
  educational opportunities of, 6
  Latinx, 33–35
  racialization and, 5–6
survival, to resistance, 110–111
suspensions, 6
systemic change, 54–57
systemic oppression, 114

tax, unrecognized, xiv–xv
teacher activist groups, 99–102
teacher education, 29, 35–43,
  150–153
teachers/teachers of Color
  activism of, 99–102, 148, 155
  anti-Muslim sentiments against,
    27
  backgrounds of, 29
  coalitions of, 131–136
  as commodities, 82–83
  current context of, 10–13
  defined, 18–19

demographics of, 11–12
historical presence of, 7–10
justice-oriented, 86, 88, 118, 156
male, 48–49, 96
racial condonement by, 32–33
solidarity and, 106–110
truths of, 156–157
Teach for America (TFA), 51
technology, lack of, 104
tenure, statistics of, 72
testing, standardized, 43, 153
training, 135
trauma, 55

unions, 103–106

vision, 67–72, 90

white students, 11, 30, 35, 40–42,
  46
white supremacy, 118, 150
white teachers
  dominance of, 96–97
  professional hiring and promotion
    of, 56, 100
  racism of, 2, 6, 9, 31, 38–39, 45,
    88, 95, 108, 133–134
(W)holeistic Science Pedagogy
  (WSP), 118–119
women, as Black teachers, 118
World Cultures Day, 133–134

Youth Participatory Action Research
  (YPAR), 127, 130
youth research, 125–131